Narrative Poems II

Vladimír Holan

Narrative Poems II

Translated from Czech by
Josef Tomáš and Katarina Tomas

Published 2010 by arima publishing

www.arimapublishing.com

ISBN 978 1 84549 416 2

© Vladimír Holan estate, c/o Aura-Pont, 2010
© Translation: Josef Tomáš, Katarina Tomas, 2010
© Illustrations: Jaroslav Šerých, 2010
© Foreword: Jiří Brabec, 2010

All rights reserved

This book is copyright. Subject to statutory exception and to the provisions of relevant collective licensing agreements, no part of this publication may be reproduced, stored in a retrieval system or transmitted, in any form or by any means, without the prior written permission of the author.

Printed and bound in the United Kingdom

Typeset in Palatino 10/16

This book is sold subject to the conditions that it shall not, by way of trade or otherwise, be lent, re-sold, hired out or otherwise circulated without the publisher's prior consent in any form of binding or cover other than that which it is published and without a similar condition including this condition being imposed on the subsequent purchaser.

arima publishing
ASK House, Northgate Avenue
Bury St Edmunds, Suffolk IP32 6BB
t: (+44) 01284 700321
www.arimapublishing.com

*This translation has been kindly subsidized
by the Ministry of Culture of the Czech Republic*

Cover and Illustrations

The Czech artist Jaroslav Šerých (1928), is a man of many talents: painter, illustrator, printmaker, sculptor, creator of monumental mosaics and of small bronze reliefs.

He graduated from The School of Applied Arts in Jablonec nad Nisou (1949), the School of Jewellery Design in Turnov (1950) and the Academy of Fine Arts in Prague (1955). He first exhibited with the group M 57 and is a member of the Society of Graphic Artists Hollar. His work is represented in the Czech National Gallery in Prague, in most of the Czech regional galleries, the New York Public Library, the National Gallery Washington, the Staatliche Kunstsammlungen Dresden, in the Vatican collection of modern art and in private collections at home and abroad.

He has received numerous awards for book illustrations: the Loisirs-Jeuenes Award in Paris (1970), the prize Premio Graphics in Bologna (1977) and the Rudolf II Prize for Fine Arts in Prague (2003).

To mark the artist's 80th birthday, a retrospective of Šerých's work opened at Prague's Museum of Fine Arts in spring 2008. In October 2008, Šerých was awarded the Czech Presidential Medal of Merit.

Contents

	Page
Foreword	9
Homecoming	15
Simply	31
A Farewell	43
Ode to Joy	49
A Nocturne	55
It Rained	63
Susannah in the Bath	71
Martin of Orle, Yclept Mortmain	89
Death comes to Fetch the Poet	99
A Letter	111
Escape to Egypt	121

Foreword

> "Unconstrained, you won't glide
> from fate to fate or age to age"
> Vladimír Holan

This collection of Holan's narrative poems, Narrative Poems II, was published in 1963, but the poems were written between 1948 and 1953, during some of the cruellest years after the establishment of a totalitarian regime in Czechoslovakia. Writing in "a delirious seclusion" in what today is regarded a legendary house on the island of Kampa in Prague, the poet experienced "all the horrors" of the late 1940s and early 1950s. Holan, in recollecting those years, emphasised that his poetry did not have a direct connection to any particular events of that time. His concern was always: "man, man's drama, man's human fate and the ill-fated heritage that he must at all times live with." Nevertheless, that particular era did instil into Holan's poetry both an urgency to portray humanity's woes, as well as an intense affinity with "the stories" of ordinary people and outcasts, who manage to preserve the integrity of their personalities in spite of the tremendous pressures of their daily life.

At the beginning of the 1930s, Holan wrote this aphorism: "existence is redoubled by threat". All the characters in Narratives Poems II are being threatened or crushed by external pressures, which are, however, difficult to decipher. Their stay in this world is viewed through the spectrum of pain because, according to Holan, "ignorance of life, is an ignorance of pain". Even though earlier in his career Holan resorted to pamphletary protests, there is no such external gesture in Narratives Poems II. This hater of positivism and of modern "certainties" was always fascinated by the mystery of human fate. Thus in his fateful poetic dramas, "he certifies mystery with his vision".

The sculptor August Rodin once wrote that a true artist must always collide with "a boundless unknowability that surrounds, on all sides, the tiny realm of the known … Some artists grimly injure their forehead on this barrier …" Holan was such an artist. The greatest mystery for him was always man, whose fate seemed to be controlled by chance, which tampered with his life and his death. And, it was this encounter with "the never-ending patience of human tribulation" that merged the poet with the unknown "others" of his poems. He was one of them and, yet, he was the one who endured the grief of those "others". "The knowledge of events means nothing to him ... if it concerns knowledge, then it is the knowledge of the heart".

In Holan's epical-lyrical and epical works from the wartime years (such as Narrative Poems I, which include The First Testament, Terezka Planetová, and The Trail of a Cloud), two types of heroes appear: a competent, complete man who is not detached from his basic values and a maiden who radiates beauty and purity. We also meet them in Narrative Poems II: a seventy-year-old man who narrates how his father carted stones for the construction of The National Theatre (a building considered to be representative of the Czech national myth) and a twenty-year-old servant girl who "was simply rejoicing and giving away her joy". The beauty Dora Závětová and the gamekeeper Martin of Orle, yklept Mortmain, constitute a similar pair. The characters are portrayed as internally complete and unbroken, as if to demonstrate, in radical contradiction, that the man who lacks order can be misused and alienated from himself. Holan's "heroes" reveal not only their deeply stored experiences of life's cruelty and injustice, but also – and this above all – the ambiguity and immeasurability of human existence. (For, as Holan writes: "It is not life that is at stake, but existence"). Those who are the simplest amongst the simple carry within themselves a desire for beauty and joy; they want to be useful or live in defenceless happiness, but are constantly confronted by a merciless world. "An orphan-virgin, a prefiguration of life" dies, and Dora, "A virgin! God's masterpiece", suffers long years of her Calvary after losing all joy and all sense of her existence.

In Narrative Poems II, Holan never concerns himself with creating a colourful plot or an attractive sequence of events. Instead, he attempts to create a paramount situation from which a simple action can unfold and deepen the consequences of the initial "incident" on which the story is based. At other times, a recollection becomes the means for a perpetual demonstration of the ambiguous role man plays in his world; or, an epical element is positioned in the background, enabling an expansion of the meditative parts. All the poems are carried along by an always-present fear about man's nature: "For the virtue of his love, a poet must view the world only through his tears ..." Holan comes from a generation of poets who believed in a meaningful world and in man's integrity; they possessed, therefore, a subtle sense of how

FOREWORD

unstable human existence really is. Holan himself had stated on several occasions that a poet's lot is "to liberate". On the one hand, there is the poet who has a real – albeit disturbed – image of man yearning for the realization of his humanity, his love and his human potential; on the other hand, there is the poet who sets forth into the domain of collapsed dreams where, instead of life, he finds the idle stagnation and emptiness of a senseless world.

In Narrative Poems II, Holan chose the type of narration from which everything that is ornate, forced or abstract is eliminated. Lacking forcefulness, the simplicity of his verse is closer to prose. This impression is enhanced by a rich and open factualness, conveying the magic of ordinary things and situations in life. The role of the narrator is decisive in his texts. The poet either encounters the participant of an action, or he narrates the story himself, but the attentive and humble participation of the narrator on the portrayed fates always dominates: "The hot-tempered heart of a poet / throbs, above all, in short stories; / his sympathy pays in bloody sweat / for every pennyworth fate, / and when the soul is called / by the most simple things, / he is already near to them, with them, *dutiful* ..." These are the kind of confessions that find – or expect to find – an attentive listener. The focal point of the stories (reinforced by returning motives, refrains, parallel concepts and anaphors) is incessantly accompanied by relatively self-contained deviations of a meditative nature. These "deviations" enlarge and, concurrently, deepen the space in which the characters move. Consequently, the narration is freed from both a conversational style, which would have diluted the work by paying too much attention to detail, and from a documentary style, with its emphasis on the authenticity of a story at any cost. The symbolic level is balanced by the testimonial, which frequently props itself up by aphorisms and catch-cries: "when platitude blooms, a miracle is already sprouting ..."; "It's best to see things from afar! he said. The more delicate a curtain, the more dust it collects!" Holan wipes away the differences between the metaphorical and the non-metaphorical form: what we would normally take for a direct appellation is, in fact, a metaphor. Valéry, a poet whom Holan admired, made an interesting observation about just that: "a clear sentence – 'Open this door!' – becomes unclear when someone addresses us the same way out in the fields".

The first edition of Narrative Poems II immediately sold out. That success represented a triumphal return of a poet who had been banned in Czechoslovakia for many years. At a time when the manifestative representations of communist ideas still ruled, Holan introduced a different perspective, which turned its attention to human fate, to simple things and to people who had been pigeon-holed. He wrote: "I clearly comprehend today how a well-trodden path, a mother's thimble or her grave can drag you down from mere wordplay to the tragic voice of a certain little valley…"

Jiří Brabec

In memory of my mother

Homecoming

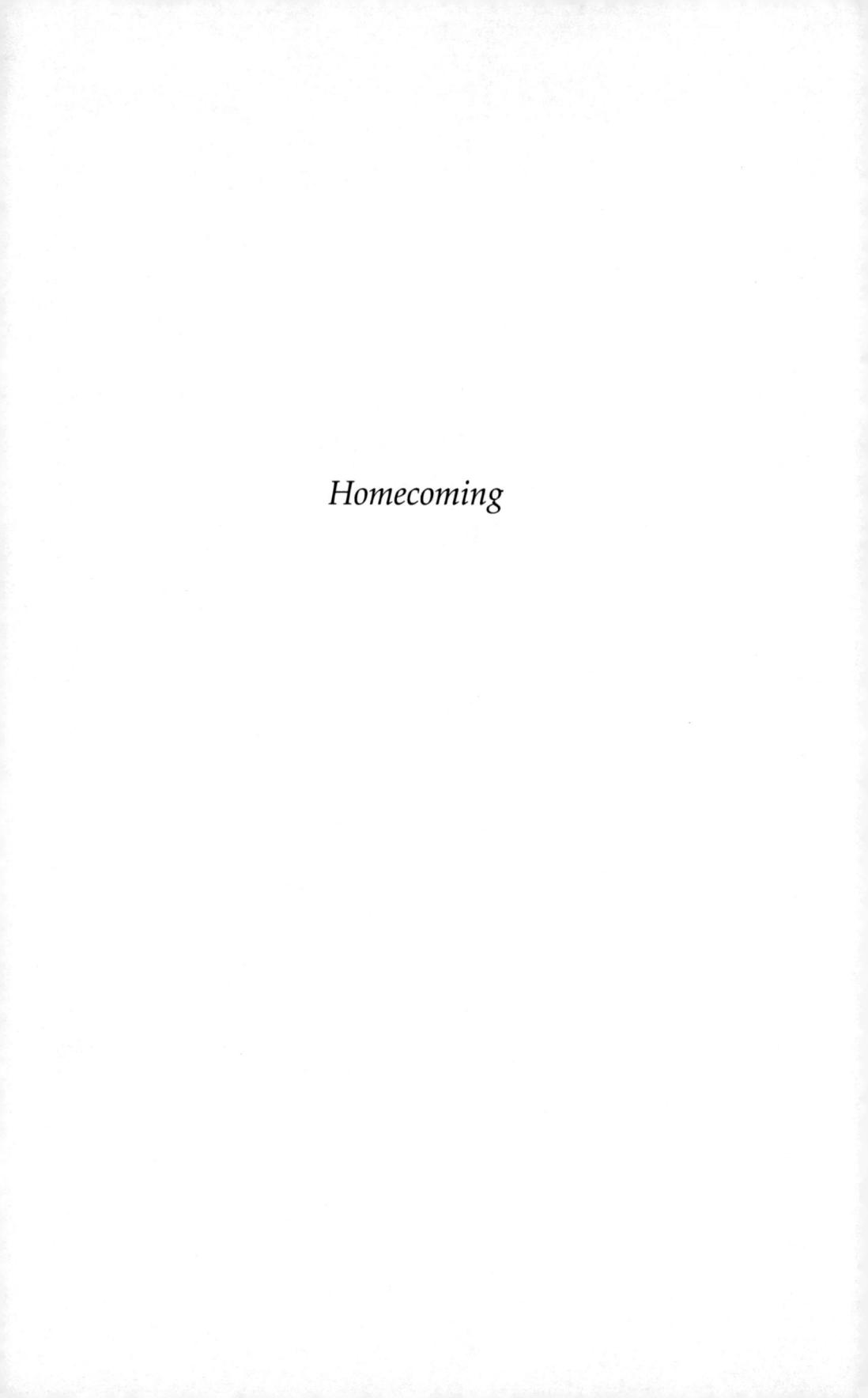

HOMECOMING

A cloud, a rumpled cloud … And yet, pitiable
for as it blew it's abdominal curtain asunder,
the land below, though it was roughly pounded,
had been long ago devoured by daily intricacy …

The wind and wolf's droppings, the heather and boulders,
combed by thistles, and a measure of oats
upturned by a cow onto fallow fields –
and only one monkish baldhead of a fountain,
only one verdure, creased into the paper with a graveyard watermark,
and only one road to the village, which was at wit's end …

Just now, a human being strides along this road.
If a youth is tempted by water from many wells,
a man longs for a spring … The one here
(in his very gait, which stoops down and almost kneels) is man.
And, in his very appearance, he is a foreigner,
who feels ashamed of being here.
And yet, he is also a native in his very shyness,
with which he smoothes his hair,
and with which he compares the handwriting
from his long past childhood
with the galley proofs of what he feels now …

Yes, he is a native … But his loneliness
is so childishly alone that it changes everything convivial
into a fear of adults and
into a fear of oaks, in whose crowns parasitic mistletoe dwells –
and when he reaches the village green, he, evil-eyed, bypasses
his natal cottage with its one perspiring window,
onto which he used to write with his finger, and with the dew of which
he used to wash out his sickly eyes … But, he well sees
that nothing has changed. At the tavern
(where, to this day, blokes have always swooped
like flies to beer; lumberjacks
in trousers made of hole-proof leather known as devil's skin,
in the coarsest of trousers but with brand name Mode de Paris buttons),
he can still read a graffito:
"All strolling companies are prohibited
from staying at this place (except on Saint's day)

under a penalty of five hundred crowns. The assigned place
is near the cemetery." ... Nothing has changed:
the almshouse is still here, as is the not dissimilar
box of the vanished shoe-boy;
the stony knife's edge of the mill still slices through bags of dog's cough,
and near the school it reeks once again of soapsuds and slops,
splashed out into Saturday's dust, in which wriggles
a blindworm or a cyclist's buckle ...

He hadn't been here for twenty years ... Now he crossed the village green
to catch up with himself at the little gate to the cemetery ...
It grates, just as it had then;
it squeaks as if the rust wanted to complain
about being disturbed by hardly anyone. And truly,
even before you enter, you can smell the *inviting* scent of flowers.
But, for the dying flowers to smell *like that*,
they need the essential fat of the dead,
just as a perfumer needs lard to produce perfume ...

He entered ... And the first falling leaflet
became his dismissory letter. But, simultaneously noticing
the wrought-iron crosses, he tearfully deemed it to be a smith's apron,
and, emboldened, he stepped forward.
His heart was indeed pounding ...
He knew too much about the game of tug-o-war
between the woeful and the others;
he knew about the toss of a horse's head
between the curve of the Diamond fields and that of the rattle-snake;
he knew about the springs in the desert and as a lighthouse keeper
he knew also about whales' lice and the sperm of goldfish;
he was familiar with the Assyrian drizzle that falls during ursine hibernation
and from the wars, he remembered a child hanging from a meat hook ...

Yet, *his* childhood was here, and here somewhere
his *mother* was also resting ... Mother and childhood –
at one time pitilessly lovelorn,
after he hardened his heart into the hammer of adventure.

At first, the black lithograph of silence confused him in that place
where a blackbird and thrush had once screeched;

HOMECOMING

it confused him so far as to convince him
that the over-sensitive grave digger had poisoned the birds ... Then he hoped
repentance would at least send something via the ravens,
who, by unclenching their claws even a little bit,
would drop at least a symbol, a sign of forgiveness ...

Mother! How you pestered her! And you pestered her so much,
as though your devil lacked angelic balance!
Just remember how year after year, always early in the morning
on the twenty-third of December, she kneaded the dough for Christmas
    twists!
(You only slept because of *her* silence.) And after the dough had risen,
she took a clothes basket and slipped the dough
between two feather quilts, so it wouldn't catch a cold, and then she carried it
to a far-flung village where they had a large baker's oven. After all,
Christmas twists baked in a baker's oven are mellower than those from
    a kitchen stove! ...
And remember how, years later, she saw you off
at a pitiful railway station (we barely made it then
because the duke's gardener held us back: "Correct, madam;
but these here are the sped-up gladioli and no one
believes me that I cut them as early as the tenth of May!") –
she walked in her bodice, a sleeveless bodice, with the suitcase
we let her carry on her back.
Oh, how she had impressed it into your heart to hold your ticket
in your fist the whole trip, so no one would wrench it from you!
And how later, we let her sweep
through all the pawn-shop chimneys,
so she could send us letters heavy with something,
even if written in hairline script.
So she could send us poppy-seed cakes,
and new shirts, and new mittens and sweaters,
and fresh kisses for Job at the very moment he wanted to hang himself;
kisses full of freshness, not vague ones that could have suited anybody;
natal kisses that could have been omens of joy,
were it not a ghost who leads us into the wasteland;
motherly kisses that finally made you kneel, though you kneeled
like an elephant, reluctantly and with a heavy heart, but like an elephant
who accepts the burden, who accepts the burden of love ...

VLADIMÍR HOLAN

You took and did not give … It's always the same:
as if Maria Magdalene were battling for us
because these were her indiscernible,
unacknowledged, pint-sized and heart-warming,
day-to-day and caring acts,
whose hidden and silent and selfless validity,
to this day, attests that we haven't perished in the gutter,
and that we may still seek the poet's stone …
Mother! We thought that she would live to her nine-hundred and thirtieth
    year …

A son, her son, now leans back against an ancient tree near the northern wall,
near the wall of the self-murderers … It is a weeping tree,
and it isn't a coincidence that it is also known as the tree of paradise …

Children, they can still see and therefore can still play blind man's bluff,
but we, our eyes sewn shut with golden tinsel,
fumble through life, painfully and yet incessantly, not suspecting
that we've merely been groping for the pages of an obituary
written in Braille …

What is not a grave? This here, for example:
it had sunk long ago beneath the weight of the lichen and
had expired like the moon's craters;
it was so sunken that one would gladly scatter it about
as though it were a mole hill,
and, in the next moment, it would become vacant
and one could dwell in it.
It has no name – so much the better for everyone!

And the neighbouring one? Nothing but a level plain. Perhaps it is
the grave of the woman who four-hundred years ago wrote a letter,
a letter that to this day has not yet arrived …

And the neighbouring one? It is newly laid, brash, and you realize
before the letter will arrive, death may overrun the one who wrote it,
or the one to whom the letter had been addressed …

And the neighbouring one? This is a substantial grave,
from its red hue to its hammed-up porphyry;

HOMECOMING

a grave of a rich man, who made himself an ashtray from the slippers of
   poesy.
A guest at his palace had walked from one heavy room to another
until, awearied, he was glad when chance
opened a secret door to the kitchen for him.
In these rooms, Pelleas and Melisanda
and Melisa and Dolcerina played
while you, during an evening feast, enjoyed
gluing candles to the stairs so that you could better see
the shoes, legs and thighs of the ascending women –
while, in the left wing, a chambermaid
tickled the heels of the mistress of the house with bristles of barley
or else with a funeral crest, which had beautified the horses at Hamlet's
   funeral …

And another grave, a grave with a photograph
(how long are you here for? and the photograph says: for a moment!),
a grave with a photograph and the name: Charlotte Painter!
I had known her once, you heartbreakingly tell yourself;
how matter-of-factly she used to turn mud into lunch for her dolls!
Why, she was your schoolmate, a good-looking girl,
who, out of mere sprightliness, showed you the dress
she would wear on Corpus Christi day, only to wear a different one!
How is this possible? Where is her spoken word,
where are her girl's shoes, where is her laced bodice, ere life reached
that age-old tragedy between Mr. Barterer and Miss Bartered?
Where are those passionate stockings of hers?
(And truly, we are more likely to first ask about things,
rather than about the dead who left those things behind,
because those things may still exist somewhere:
in father's cardigan, a dash of tobacco;
left behind by the engineer, railway tracks rusting on red sand,
tracks that were supposed to end in the sea;
left behind by the consumptive, not a picture but a coat beddabled with
   Turner's yellow;
down-at-heel shoes left behind by the waiter who used to make
lotuses from napkins at wedding receptions;
left behind by the poet, a paperback edition of debts;
left behind by the child, a rattle or a lock of hair;
left behind by the strike-breaker [who became famous by calling the strike of

strike-breakers],
the trumpet of a bugler, whom we provoked at an overblown performance
by eating a lemon or a cucumber in front of him;
left behind by the sinner, a coal mine and a hospice for twelve of the poorest;
left behind by the excellent cook, nothing because she didn't believe in
    a rolling pin
and used her fist to tenderize beefsteaks;
left behind by the wood-carver, a wood-worm – the very heart of a wooden
    marionette –
and left behind by the seamstress, invariably a sewing machine presser foot
continually pierced by a needle …)

And here – where, as if wafting from a confectioner's flower shop, a draft
fills your nose with the sweet scent of Crocus, Lady's Mantle and Fly Agaric –
here rests, from one new moon to the next, the one
whom we used to call, I no longer know why: Hepe!
He was a hunt beater and was shot 'by mistake'.
The bad and ill-tempered painter's glue of your memory flakes off,
and you invoke the distorted image three times with the sign of a cross …

False tears charm the graveyard slugs!
And truly, at the next grave
you must recall those villagers
who, after sizing up the pastries,
tearfully rejoiced when Josef Wantitso
died with the Lord … An eccentric or a scum?
To his wedding he wore galoshes because he couldn't afford patent-leather
    shoes …
When his beloved horse perished, he had its head boiled
and always kept it on his desk …
He used to say: "It's curious, but be it an orphan's or a widow's tune,
our folk will unrelentingly turn it into a dancing tune,
and yet they deny me the right to soak my bread in brandy.
I regret, I really do, that one time at a winter feather-stripping
(when outside the birds shiver and the only thing that's quiet
is the feather duster for sweeping out soot),
I wanted to warm a bottle of red wine
on the belly of a woman lying in childbed … People, however,
know well how to talk, but they talk badly, and I know

HOMECOMING

that in heaven God placed Christ on His right side
and that, therefore, not only is Christ's left hand closest to Him,
but so is Christ's heart ..."

But, let us depart from the trunk of the weeping tree
and keep fumbling along! ... It will be just another grave:
the man and his drama ... Wenceslas Sibun.
It suffices if you search for something in your pocket
and the post horse, the old beggar, will come to you
as far as the footpath ... Similarly,
death had once been searching for something and Wenceslas had rushed to
    her ...
He took a tram to its terminal station and back again
because, as he said, lunch would anyhow still be hot,
and as he was disembarking, a certain motorcycle disturbed his visit
    into town.
On the cross you read: Road-mender. But it is rumoured
that he was a "ladder-climber". That, after he had gone grey
and after it had gone dark, he used to peep through windows
to watch copulating couples.
Not through the ground-floor windows, where the curtains were usually
    drawn,
but through those on the first floor,
for which he needed to put up a ladder.
And for that he endured many beatings –
they even burnt his ladder, but he always found a new one ...

O life, wherein people judge cruel passions,
so they can secretly possess much crueller ones themselves!
O life, wherein people have hearts of flint,
but still you won't strike a spark off them!

Children, they can see and therefore can play blind man's bluff,
but we, our eyes sewn shut with horse-hair,
fumble our way through life,
obdurately and yet incessantly, not suspecting
that we've merely been groping about
for the pages of an outlaws' record
written in Braille ...

And indeed, here is different dead woman:
like the promise of a single certainty,
a certainty not limited to a level or a stacked measure,
but one that is abundant and therefore is descending ... Whereto?
Upward or downward? Question everything that hasn't been adjudged
    to you,
but don't ask anything of this marriageable girl,
who had been deranged by country lads as far as suicide's servitude ...
You're well acquainted with the River Iser and its "horse trenches",
a frozen cornet and cherubic swallowing ...
It was noon ... A Slovak was drinking meths,
denaturised alcohol ... And he was looking but wasn't moving,
even though his pulse was beating like a flee beneath the bandage of a boxer,
whose gloves were filled with lead ... And she walked,
walked silently to the river, although she wore wooden shoes on her feet.
Her name was Agnes ... And, as she was drowning – and she was irritated
almost to anger by the wet transformation of her skirt, which was
made of printed calico from Kosmonosy – she couldn't distinguish whether
the cross she had been cleaning
with sawdust from a spittoon was made of gold or silver,
yet hollow it had been ...

But, let us move on! You read: Albert, gamekeeper. Yes,
one of the world's great disdainers ... an Anchorite ... His letterbox box
he used as a box for toilet paper.
And once, during the new moon, he shot dead your father's dog
and sent him the collar with these words: "You mustn't do that,
otherwise I'll arrive bare-arsed on a shoe polish box!"

And here lies a miller's journeyman from the mill Lobsterich,
who was pulled down by a water sprite at Posen's weir!

And here lies the one who lost his farmstead in a lawsuit
because of a single boundary stone called Stayinplace;
he has as his neighbour the grave of a shire poet,
whose name these days was John Headbreaker,
and whom a micro-pegasus had always faithfully accompanied.
But, even he recognized human praise and preferred, therefore,
his kidneys to be fried in Dionysian wine ...

HOMECOMING

And his neighbour is a gipsy king,
his fiddles nailed to a woodless board
with nails torn out from the coffin-maker's coffin.

And his neighbour is Constantine Brolbs, the smith.
Although, there was a constant drip from the roof of his working forehead,
and although he constantly drank herbs,
there was such a frost inside of him that it would have frozen
even a calf inside a heifer's belly.
And yet, he, too, had a longing, a longing to be buried
in a coffin made from an oak that had been struck by lightning.
Since nowhere in the shire could they find precisely such a tree
(oh, they didn't overly exert themselves!), and since the last will
of the poor is never fulfilled, they buried him in a bag ...

And his neighbour is the grave of a soldier from the Napoleonic times
with this alarming inscription: SIMPLY RABIDLY, oh yes:
SIMPLY MADLY ... with even some houseleek sprouting from it.

And his benevolent companion is Eve Wonderling.
You can still hear her screaming through an open window:
"Compresses, yes! Death, no!" And then:
"Mama, one skein is four balls, is it not?"
It happened between the two feasts of St. Mary,
as she entered her seventeenth year and
one week later she was to be married,
but then she caught typhoid fever ... Even before her temperature had risen
they already placed a candle in her hand ... Then she died ...
But, even if she had pulled through, sir,
all her hair would have fallen out!

And this one here, she had once been a beauty who'd worn perforated
    stockings
to match her complexion, which resembled a flying brimstone butterfly;
later she became a harlot with her pillow in the window,
to underscore, as the saying goes,
that her own is better than ours –
and then she became a martyr whose heart
(like the bang of an auctioneer's gavel over the last of the charms)
tried in vain to deafen the bellowing of jazz

from pastures grazed-down by the gasbags of civilization –
who of you, gathering in the retina of Jesus Christ,
like Sodom's reflection, will throw the first stone at her?!

And this one here is a widow, whose husband had been stricken by
    the plague.
She had walked behind his coffin wearing a fumigated veil,
and yet she died soon after anyway ...

And her neighbours are children, many children!
An articulated chain of children and the small bones of fledglings,
after fate's wild geese had chilled the eggs ...
And children born out of wedlock, eaglets thrown
into a hat of sphinx-like insults ...
And children born before the harrowing wedding ceremony,
or after the wedding, but who were hauled into nothingness
just as they were cutting their first teeth ...
And juvenile stingers and virginal wax,
and sunrays that are unbespoken, caves that are unbetrothed
but are hauled into nothingness by the Fates' whirling spindles,
hauled to such depths that you need an excavation map
to follow the insane weaver ...

And a pregnant self-murderess, who weeps over two deaths
into the scarf with which they bound that quivering little chin of hers ...

And another self-murderess (the clothesline was sufficient for her),
who makes you ponder whether suicide is profane, since
children are killed wilfully by diseases
and precisely then, when even a marionette feels compassion ...

And a woman in childbed, without soup, bread or a sip of wine,
whom fate had mixed in among the grits,
and who was, in her exiled state, devoured by the swine ...

And a stone on the grave of the confessor for the hanged,
who found it repugnant to eat pork necks
but liked the verticality of lambs' tails ...

And a monument for a student for whom every line turned into a circle,

HOMECOMING

and the first circle was the ghastly circle of hell:
the genitalia of a danseuse who didn't know whether to raise her leg
    or not …
He locked himself in for one and a half turns and then he did it …

And a monument for a chaplain with the inscription: Diis Manibus!
To the underground gods! who, he alleged, were far fewer
than the number of commentators on the fourth eclogue of Virgil …

And here is a grave that whispers: I used to give alms
because I killed. And another grave that complains:
I used to give no alms, I only sinned.
And a third grave that laughs: Ergo, go and kill,
so the poor can fare a little better …

No, not even children can see, which is why they can play blind man's bluff,
while we, with our mouldering brain weeping,
blindly fumble through life and distrustfully evade love.
All the while we're groping for the pages in borrowed books,
with our eyes sewn shut with paper string
and, like the nude to the naked, we carry paper wreaths to the dead.
Sleep sweetly! we say on borrowed time, and then we go to bed …
You, who have not departed yet and whose head so far hasn't been disturbed
by the circular ground plan of history,
you finally reach the mortuary,
where grey draws towards violet, like a donkey towards a thistle.
Through a single window you behold a definite inattentiveness
that surrounds the world's last little chamber … Here only drudgers
bronze the air, much like excrement lines a lavatory …
The Easter rattle of forever-clenched teeth
will draw your attention to a dead man lying on a slab
and to the governor of Worms, who rises up
and in the folds of pus values himself for money …
The cake is poisoned, look out! his relatives had warned him,
but they told him after it was all inside of him,
along with the savings book from the orphans' bank …

It's sweet to be alive! But we, like racoons,
wash our lump of sugar far too long in life's waters,
until nothing remains …

VLADIMÍR HOLAN

We are ciphers and we are pick-pocketed;
we don't need to do a headstand for everything,
which we don't have, to fall out of us ... We, with our untidy
knot of angina pectoris;
we, who ask in an embryonic manner what for do we live;
we, who find no rest here, not even in our unconsciousness;
but yet also we, who advertise: *Will buy old teeth,*
unusable dentures of the deceased, straight away!;
and consequently also we, for whom everything appears already in such
    a way
that if insects were to put down roots, people would sprout up!
And it was as if God were only waiting for Satan's approval –
the selfsame God who, like God alone, has always been
far too heavy – because in His anger and in His compassion
He enjoyed using both His hands, since they were the right ones ...

But, be sombre beyond all sombreness,
and detest ever so much the bird catcher's glue for catching the nightingales:
if you glance over the graveyard wall,
you will see in the distance a beautiful greenish hill,
which is like the navel of the bottle from which lightning will drink,
and you will see a pond embankment, and you will recall
that where whilom a child poked its small finger,
today streams a brook that drives a mill ...

Why should you despair? The most extraneous of the Nonae
wasn't the ninth! Virgins still throw their bridal wreaths
onto a male tree; inside the ribcage
of the roughest woodcarving beats some sort of heart;
and the lovers of poesy – the giver of invisible blood –
they are in a certain manner worldly-blessed:
they didn't see, but they believed ...

But, the day is waning ... Perhaps a stone that's carried away inside a dog's
    mouth;
perhaps a pruned evergreen or some kind of pettiness;
perhaps a clinging to life; perhaps those mockingbirds
poisoned by the grave digger; perhaps your sins,
which transformed the wiles of time so much
that even the graveyard has been transformed ...

HOMECOMING

But, it is already late … It is already late
for love's night train, which would have stopped
between an owl's heart and the heart of a bat,
near home … Only a blind tohuvabohu,
only chaos always has enough time
to come first in our life:
wherein everything that has come first, from the very first sin,
first sob, first grief,
first telegram and first radio wave,
has been a plea for help …

What does it mean to immortalize? To look for one's mother?
Yes, to look for is, after all, already the future!
Although, to look for the grave of one's mother, among so many
unknown and recognized graves, and not to find it
and not be capable of imagining even her face,
means to be able to comprehend humbleness only after our heart bursts –
all at once naked, alone and without fate!

(1948)

Simply

SIMPLY

We met towards the end of September
when the trees are brought back to life
by a kind of disembodiment, a kind of expiry,
and when the air, traced by smooth or sharp senses,
waits for a soul to paint
with the silent observance of a long past storm.
We stood outside the tobacconist's and some of us
had small change and some had none ...
On the storefront was a notice:
This shop is for sale. Someone had scrawled under it
in chalk: FOR BUGGER ALL!
We looked at it a while and then
walked to the pub.

"I am," he said (but he said it like a humming bough,
with its music suddenly fractured by the bursting forth of a pause),
"over seventy already; every ladder reaches its end, sir! ...
But, I do like to imbibe in wine ... Just look here
at this: how it strikes the glass, merges with it,
permeates it ... How one's hand suddenly has blood on it ...
Yesterday I went on a pilgrimage to St. Ludmila.
To laugh or to cry? Heads or tails?
A car arrived at the church with two priests in it,
and those priests got dressed bashfully in that car
before marching at the head of a procession. A fiddler,
a drummer, an accordionist and two saxophonists followed them.
Oh, for the love of Pete! I didn't recognize what they were blowing,
but some driveller claimed it was the Congo-cocktail ...
Heads or tails, to cry or to laugh?
I am over seventy already; when they erected
the bridge at Zavist near Prague, I was *the first* to walk across it!
Time, they say ... Now, along the lines of tomorrow morning
      I will wake up:
I'm delivering this as a prophesy. Time, they say,
but we always manage to fade away long before we know
what it is that will never desert us; indeed,
even before our fading has begun –
which should be an upgrowth – we mistakenly open the trap door ..."

I didn't ask him anything, but he nodded

and, looking down at me like the sun on Candlemas Day,
he went on: "We'd have to make use of a well shaft for the candle,
so as to see what a weeping eye is. But
our compassion is inexperienced. A mere impression:
we close down our judgement but, in truth, without the force
of a closing wound. A mere excess: we emanate events and episodes.
Any pettiness that is lined with feeling:
and alas, we impose our whole heart's substance and meaning upon it! ...
I enjoy recollecting now ...
I am empty, and the well's windlass works ...
I enjoy recollecting my childhood now ... As a poet,
you surely give precedence to a worthless ornament over a false one,
and you love pointlessness, which is at the heart of every game ...
Without agonizing over the question of what poesy is:
whether Carmen magicum, vinum daemonum or a crying shame,
I enjoy recollecting now, even if today
we are disarrayed, nay disarranged,
as though we had to make room for what is approaching ...
Perhaps too, we have been banished elsewhere,
in the same way that grownups cast out children
for talking about matters that are too profound or bold ...
It is with his truth, after all, that
an old man deceives a child when he asks
what flowers it received from the spirits of the departed
or when he claims that the unceasing number
of fluttering butterflies reminds him of a single caterpillar.

Partial flames promise completeness,
but it is the smoke that fulfils it.
The smoke of my memory is substantial ...
Sometimes I have a different impression: the river
stayed in its course, and it was the trees that floated away ...
Or: the clearest reminiscence and still it obscures the present time ...

Please, did you notice at the entrance
to this tavern a display cabinet with the inscription:
PRODUCTS OF THE BLIND ...?"
_____

I hadn't noticed it; for as we entered,

SIMPLY

the barmaid's shadow fell upon my heart.
Besides, at our midnight, the clock struck only eight o'clock.
And the truth is, our wine glasses seemed so forlorn
that we pulled off our wedding rings and ordered a new bottle.
And I, filled with a yearning lost within his destiny,
asked him to continue his narration ...

"It's best to see things from afar!" he said. "The more delicate
a curtain, the more dust it collects!" And with the island
of his hand, he smoothed the floodtide of his still-plentiful hair.
His whiskers were jovial too, like those of Taras Bulba.
"You know, whenever I think of people ... I invariably picture a man,
a man escaping through an immovable beast.
If he sometimes stops, it's only
to light a cigarette or to appear as a face
that knows it's being photographed ...

I see those faces, I see their momentary stupefaction;
I see it all the more clearly and ominously, the more
space disincarnates, and this precisely then when time sins ...
There was jealousy, which gripped hold of our instincts until rigor mortis
    set in.
There were flat tones, those excellent illuminators
of pre-arranged music ... There is a girl,
who used to forgive before someone insulted her.
There is joy, destroyed by gratitude.
There is a spade and a crest, and there are twins
who dug their grave solely with that crest of theirs.
And there are babies: you, who used to wonder, be astonished!
And there are murderers and misgivings, saving themselves
by the extravagant elopement of their heart ...
And there will be enough heart for the soul ... Be patient,
or we shall go with our glass to the grape
that's just being pressed ...

I don't know how to narrate and I fear deceitful correctness,
and I no longer know what is sombre or what is dark;
but then, even an India-ink line doesn't know ...

It is possible that we only met today
so that I could tell you about an altogether trifling incident:
this incident." (And here his voice thawed;
and if so far he had been unburdening himself, he now was confiding,
and he began to shiver, and he seemed to be apologizing,
and he seemed to feel that whenever the soul assimilated walls,
it wasn't so that we climbed over them.)

"My parents built a small house and, aside from the roofer,
they did everything themselves ... My mother was a simple woman.
Wherein she wasn't a rose, she was a flower.
With her long braid, wound three times around her head,
she lamented with joy and revelled in her singing.
She used to say: 'Yes, life! For a miracle it's enough,
but for a word it's too little!' ... Once she told me
(and only today do I understand that she was really speaking to you):
'When you meet him, tell him that I don't know
if it's his curiosity that makes him constantly think about death –
and he thinks about it with a passionate needfulness.
But, tell him that surely it's his fear of death
that awakens malice within him ... He deceives himself,
but I'll keep praying for him ...'

My father Joachim (less humble and more excessive
rather than contradictory, and thus somewhat surly)
wavered over such a confession, but
he equally hated any deliberate pathos: a wall
split apart by everything coerced from a torture chamber,
or a museum's interior consumed by the statuary.
He was poor and owned next to nothing.
He had a beard like those sailors who had once
strummed the tow ropes
of Sir Raleigh's gluttonous argosies;
he was miserably kind and had hands
that revealed a calloused permit
to the guardian fire of drudgery;
after a hangover, he sometimes delighted
in bruised reminiscences about floriated crockery ...
'We are beggars,' he said, 'and all others are
like dogs who gnaw on a waterfall and then micturate all day ...'

SIMPLY

The ash from his cigarettes seasoned his hot-tempered words.
Sometimes, a whole village of images resided inside of him,
which altered if left to run their course
and warped if utilized. In a word:
one nonsensical sentence and all was saved.
I can still see the obtuse angle of his elbow's extent
and how his palm propped up, under the weight of Absalom's hair,
his distinctive face, which quivered within this parable's teardrop.
'Listen my boy,' he said, 'from a fallen tree
to a fallen leaf it is only a few short steps …'
We sometimes fell an oak to prop up a Sweet William.
But, only man's death reveals to us the most fundamental
of his concealed being, like a tree that reveals its roots
only after it's been uprooted …'

Back then, I remember, we'd had lechery for lunch:
some pea and barley gruel, which exuded
a human acidulousness throughout the front room,
not unlike that from feather quilts laid out in the sun …
Father's tobacco burnt faster than paper …
People, too, in those days went by rather dismal names:
Hiddenly, Croaker or Wainmouth
who, in the presence of God, had at one time been a carcass stuffer.
They were father's friends, delivery men, "dubious" folks,
"runaways", who owned nothing, absolutely nothing.
All they had brought with them from the hills were clocks,
which they hung on bare walls and wound up regularly,
praising them whenever they chimed … One might expect
that such heavy hearts must suffer from the deepest guilt …
But no! They carted stone! And, saying little
(their words breviloquent across their lips), they went after the word,
which reversed its tracks, changing
neither its direction nor itself … At that time a biting fog
assailed everything … The autumn burned the limestone …
My father, who pursued anything to join the roots
so they would conceal the primeval forest, began to cart
marble from Slivenec for the construction of the National Theatre.
It was a glorious time then; perhaps, akin to
nowadays searching pell-mell for a house

with gas lighting, and finding it ...

Enthusiasm doesn't quest after a river with a ferryman.
Enthusiasm swims across ... My father, who was squeezed daily
through the honeycomb and out daybreak's door, harnessed up
and went straight to the quarry! ... 'Limy soil, a good soil,'
he said – and I still see the quarter-arc
carved into his forehead by the cap he'd obstinately planted on his head.
His teeth ached at that time. But he said to me:
'Whosoever does not control himself is anecdotal! People want action!'
And he cracked the whip into the twilight. His horses
he loved very much. They were two short stories bound into
a novel. When he gave them sugar and when
he unharnessed and caressed them, his hands were
as if filled with strawberries. Indeed, it was also
a mystery, which did not enquire
what it was his impatient heart so desired that his decency could
suddenly turn into ruthlessness ... This happened when he beat his horses,
the horses who might have just been suffering from colic ...
But, even the heavens let fall what they cannot carry ... It is little wonder then
that along those bone-jolting roads – on which the load
sometimes was so heavy that the reversing wagons
had to be underlaid with grave stones –
it is little wonder then that my father and his grooms
were already doleful and stopped for a gulp of white gin
at the pub, WHERE IT NEVER RAINS INTO A BARREL FULL OF RUM!

We must maintain our manners (they whispered maliciously)
so as to hold high our banners! But ah,
Maria of the Wetlands, they sure drank then; they drank
and swore like troupers, and thought of their wives and children,
and blasphemed and, whenever necessary, broke
some frailties so that they injured themselves and soon
filled the taproom with a partridge's wisdom or
with the spirit of a chicken on calves' legs ...
Towards morning (with its colours as pungent as burps after eating
    radishes),
all of them, like a single wrinkle on a lake worried by the wind,
kicked aside their chairs and went into the yard without counting
their five-hundredth grey hair ... And they went straight to Prague!

SIMPLY

'To the National Theatre!' they said, refusing everything,
much like the shipwreck at the bottom of the ocean
objects the construction of new ships …
Those were the times, were they not? Though the times were less good
for those who liked to set fire to a cathedral to warm themselves,
only to turn their back on it lest they went blind!
And now it was snowing, snowing silently,
as though only after death should one loudly utter that
which one only whispered before birth! … "

One could ask, and at the time I did ask the old man,
asked naively: "Your father carted
the Slivenec marble to Prague? Once a day?
Or how often was it? For how many years? How much
might such a load have possibly weighed? How many horses pulled it?
How old was your father then? Where did he live?
How many children did he have? When did he return home?
The road he drove along: was it good or bad?
Was the road bare or was it lined with trees on either side?
What kind of trees? Plums? How many years did your father
live to see? And where was he buried?
How long did their trip from Slivenec approximately take?
Did they take food with them? Did you sometimes ride with your father?
Did they take a dog along with them?"

He replied to my face: "There was a dog, there always was!
And also the goddess Chlipa and, wrapped in a shred of cloth,
a piece of resin for a crushed finger …
But why are you asking all this? Though, I don't know
how much darkness must perforce encircle translucence
so as to reveal it; though, I do well know
there are feelings that do not yearn to be explained –
like jealous work, which out of loneliness
possesses only shyness to defend itself with!"

Had I displeased him with my questions?

VLADIMÍR HOLAN

His voice was suddenly out of breath
and was almost screaming blue murder ... As if he were charging ahead
with a lighted candle, trying to set fire to
a butterfly in flight ...

But after another drink, he said: "Someone
full of brandy once told me that we proceed with feeling,
but we don't go down without pain ... Maybe
all our progress toward a hereafter
is a perpetual withdrawal from God's stepladder,
so that we can finally glimpse, from a more substantial vantage point,
a faithful portrait of our genesis ..."

And after one more drink, he continued: "My father
used to transport that stone from Slivenec with passion;
after all, it was for the National Theatre ... With passion, I say,
as though he'd been throwing boulders into his innermost lake
to determine how deep it was ... Imagine,
he earned sixty Kreutzer a day for that,
of which he donated, at his own behest
and willingly, six Kreutzer daily for the construction ... Look sir,
you and I are perhaps the kind of people
who will maidenly hide all sorts of personal filth,
and we'll go about it so barefacedly
that we conceal even the slightest goodness in us.
But my father was a simple man ... For him,
it was all about ardour, amazement itself, selflessness
growing wildly in love ... For him,
everything was always dawning, dawning in a way
that helped him see those stones for making pigments ...
He knew that something sublime
surpassed him, but he never felt
cast-off by the sublime
just as he never felt that something could be turned into an entity,
an entity made present by his mere presence ... You understand me! ...
Truly, the greatness of people isn't measured
by what they might have done for us had we lived in poverty,
even if we believe in effective love ...
For my father it was his inborn greatness that,
after it had entered his soul, bent down the head of his body ...

SIMPLY

And bent it towards a humble sensing,
not a sniffing, of the future and of beauty,
a beauty he was unknowingly perceiving;
indeed, he was unaware that he was blasting literary rock
with the gunpowder of his eye …

I don't know for how long he had bartered
as an adolescent, in the shire of Turnov,
his prospected agates for the inflammation of his veins.
I don't know for how long, in another place,
he foot stomped lime for bricks with the same passion
as he later foot stomped grapes in Slovakia …
I don't know for how long he had roamed along those roads,
all the roads of the Koneprus-Sivenec,
famous for its limestone …
I believe, however, that the brotherhood of suffering
is eternally transient, and that almost all of us
enter it so that we may some day be
commemorated in a poem by one of the Passionist Sisters …

And now it is she who continues her song:

When the theatre was completed and the building
resounded, con spirito, with the fingering
of the holes on a flute
and with a tragedy on every lunar eclipse,
which was as foxy as a sickle in the cornflowers –
my father, even if he was on fire and was burnt
by the wick of his impatience,
for the rest of his life never dared
to enter 'that shrine', as he used to call it …

Was it out of fear, awe, decency or timidity,
which had no desire to lick, along with Dante,
the mirror of Narcissus? … Or, simply because
a pheasant does not belong to the one who plucks its feathers
but to the one who has it as a meal? Or, perhaps
truth for him was only the stone,
which he did not dare *step on*?

Or, maybe because he (centred on his imagination)
preferred intuition to cognition?
Or, because of his quiet unpretending:
I wouldn't understand it anyhow, would I?
_ _

I don't know ... Mystery returns by reflection
everything ... Even itself ..."

(1949)

A Farewell

A FAREWELL

Come along subtle tale, come out of the chamber
wherein our hearing had barely begun to decay
when the blowfly of music flew in –
come into the night and reminisce with me,
you who knows that art is not a mere record of approximations.

It was in August, on a bench in the park.
The wind was bending tree branches as though it wanted to build a ship.
A girl, perhaps five years old, sat down beside me
and from her satchel pulled out a book ... I asked
whether it was a picture book ... Opening it she replied:
"Far from it! But look here: all those childish words!"
Then she ran off and played with a boy.
He shouted at her: "Stay!" But she kept running.
When he caught her, he urged her: "Gee, my ox!"
And she: "Gee, my little horse!" ... Before long,
the boy grumbled that he was hungry.
When she offered him a bun, he declared longingly:
"For hunger, there's sausage and bread!"

For the sake of these children and for all others, an old man stood
on the riverbank. There was nothing remarkable about him,
even his face was clean-shaven,
but the wind around him was so brisk
that he beheaded the flies with his beard ... The old man
swayed and in both hands held
about two dozen small parasols, elaborately made
out of skewers and comely printed paper
(the entire dream book of Queen of Sheba had been sacrificed for it).

The old man clutched those tiny parasols very gently –
and you understood he existed among the defenceless ...
whom fate, which urinates from its mouth, tells even before their birth:
"When you crawl out of your mother and see a rug – come out!
If you can't see it – don't bother!"
The old man clutched those little parasols almost menacingly;
they held his life's final meaning
when life was still hopeful ... So far he hadn't sold a single one ...
The old man did not simply hold those little parasols:
he embraced them, he caressed them, he invented them,

they were his idea and an infinite patience
in his already-trembling hands. He worked on them
always only during the day, when light cost next to nothing,
whereas at night he would have used a whole log of tallow
with a piece of church bell rope for the wick.
He had dreamt them out of himself and, therefore, could stand up with
    them proudly,
like someone who, from a long-past age, still rules the present moment!
Those little parasols were heavy, like the words whispered to a priest.
Those little parasols were feather-light, like the absolution of sins by a
    confessor.
Those little parasols were for children, and he loved children,
so he was incapable of selling those little parasols; he could only give them
    away ...

But a sudden wind gust crushed all the old man's frailties ...
To this day I can still see him, looking at the desolation
and whispering in confusion: "Where had I failed in my duty?"
I can still see how he hurled the lot onto the footpath
and trampled it to a pulp ... It's a wonder he didn't go mad with grief.
I felt like crying, but he put on a face eager for a fight. That is how anger,
suddenly laid bare and thereby somewhat weakened,
will throw over itself a lion's skin ... Not long after,
yet still like someone who only acts out of heavy-heartedness,
he stepped forward and leant against the railing.

Just in passing he noticed the span of the bridge, which
proved almost painfully that the iron was too tight under its arms,
so that, on his own accord, he only gazed into the river.

Suddenly he recalled how, at the funeral
for the chairman of the society for the protection of animals,
about fifty dogs had stood to attention in front of the crematorium,
and how some of the bulldogs had gold fillings
in their jaws ... And he remembered a certain moon and wondered
whether one could address it by its surname, the way his friend,
a railway-man, addressed his wife by her surname ...
And he remembered how much he loathed visiting cemeteries,
but also how an unloved road may still lead into a small chamber
where we will feel good ... And he remembered

A FAREWELL

that he was wearing a suit made from his *gravegrandmother*'s attire,
and that, whenever one dreamed about the dead, it was going to rain …
The worst clouds, the supreme rain, good water, little parasols! …
Little parasols, moon, dogs, hook with which to grab
an incoming boat or drowned men! …
And, as though out of the cloudy sky but already out of his swoon, he heard
the voice of one of the passing girls:
"I don't dye my hair, I only get a rinse!"
Yes, he said to himself: "rinses, waves, sailboat races, vests, water, little parasols! …
Water yes, but no sun, water yes, but no sun,
water, waves, water, good good water!"
_____

And, he was already at the point of bending forward … But,
he accomplished it only after nightfall.

(1949)

Ode to Joy

ODE TO JOY

It is a lovely evenfall in summer ... in summer because it is summer,
and it is quite senseless because it is lovely ... Everything is featherlight,
and everything is up above, and topmost of all
is the dance of the elephants ...

But, into my heart falls a teardrop – a teardrop that knows well
that the sea is much vaster than the earth –
and within the depths of my heart,
a long-forgotten plain girl is suddenly revived,
a servant girl who died half a century ago ...

She was twenty years old then. An orphan virgin,
a prefiguration of life, but so lacking in precedent
that even fate did not know how to deserve her love ...
Because of her contemporaries' laziness, we do not know what her eyes were
 like,
but from her contemporaries' eagerness,
I sense that her eyes were trusting and appeasing.
She was beautiful ... It was a beauty
without airs and graces; a beauty that would have remained silent
had it not, long ago, begun to sing in paradise ...
But she sang, and her singing was so immediate
that even the most trivial recollection
would have violated an innocence like hers ...
She was simply rejoicing, and since she expected nothing,
she gave away her joy to others
and thus could never encounter her self ...

It was all but impossible to catch sight of her ... It was only natural
that the men ceaselessly kept vigil over their beacon.
Whosoever could see her ... It was only natural
that the women vilified her between their thighs.
Subsequently, a certain lad, blinded by the golden bull of her virginity,
showed how even out of godlike madness
it is possible to commit a mortal sin, and he killed himself.
Old hags, those back-alley abortionists, felt insulted. And everyone else –
those with vitreous noses, so transparent
that one could see their snot and nose hair –
became enraged ... Lucy ("that whore, who so far
hadn't even ailed yet") had to leave the shire

in which even the ivy's veins had swelled with offence …

I can see her in G … She went from house to house sewing –
and each of these houses the French horn did not know
how to express it's vexation with the plaster columns –
and every Saturday afternoon she cleaned
the office at the local brewery.
She liked her work and did it humbly and silently
because she venerated mystery –
and I really do not know
why a word, a verse and a book come into existence,
or the talk of a serpent or that out of a dog's hand …

It was a lovely evenfall on a Saturday … on a Saturday because it was
    a Saturday,
and it was quite senseless because it was lovely … Everything was
    featherlight,
and everything was up above, and topmost of all
was the dance of the elephants …
Lucy entered the office, opened the windows,
and, just before she soaked the mop, she noticed
the three kings' initials above the door …

How beautiful (standing there thus) she was!
It was a beauty without airs and graces;
a beauty that would have remained silent
had it not, long, ago begun to sing in paradise …
But she sang, and her singing was so immediate
that even the most trivial recollection
would have violated an innocence like hers …
She was simply rejoicing and giving away her joy,
and thus could never encounter her self –
and, longing for a human being (the way a miracle itself longs for it),
she stepped closer to the window and looked out.

It was St. Wenceslas' day … She noticed the colchicum,
and behind the colchicum a field that was gnawed out by a brick kiln,
and, farther on, a little alley from where some boys
blew her kisses … But this time she wasn't smiling,
and she began to recall how long ago the saint's army,

ODE TO JOY

dressed in kilts trimmed with gold,
had advanced through here all night long, and how after all,
thanks to the wisdom of the duke, no battle had taken place …
Perhaps that was the only reason why we celebrate Christmas since those
    times,
she told herself, and all at once saw her mother
pouring raisins from a paper bag onto a pastry board …
Suddenly she felt childlike and thus immortal;
she was nine years old again – nine being the number of angelic choirs –
and already then she liked to sing
in accompaniment with the sweet aroma of Christmas cakes,
and once again she knew nothing about the sex of the moon,
which was painfully splaying itself open like the mouth of a gutted fish …
Sex? Yes! Several boys were calling on her now,
but her hand was too heavy
to throw her bridal wreath onto a tree –
and yet too light
to trawl her lover's face out of the hole hacked into the ice …

This dress-maker, accustomed to a bundle of pins between her teeth, now
unknowingly touched her lips,
stepped back from the window and set to work.
Fate itself, which did not know how it might deserve her love,
pulled her head towards the floor, and she, with buckets of pellucid water
that flowed from the fabulous mountains of Symplegad,
scrubbed and wiped it with the wig of a fallen angel …

Then suddenly dusk descended, descended so unexpectedly
as if a cloud had to be punished for the smallest of the sunbeams' sins …
She rose up from her knees, lit the kerosene drop-light,
and scrubbed the floor from the corners towards the middle of the room …
In that scrubbing was something of a saw
that wanted to cut the boards for a gentler floor.
In that scrubbing was something of a weaver's shuttle
that wanted to weave a carpet under the feet of Christ the Lord.
In that scrubbing was something from the heights of Chaldean astrology
that prostrated itself to the two stars of her knees.
During that scrubbing the word and love searched for one another,
and when they found each other the result was – silence …

But then, either a bluebottle fly
suddenly whirred past her eyes,
or else a far too ticklish lock of hair dropped into her face:
Lucy lashed out fiercely with her scrubbing brush
and hit the lamp above her. She smashed it,
and droplets of glowing kerosene
swarmed down her sweaty back like insects before a storm …
And she was burning and screaming … And two days later she died.

(1950)

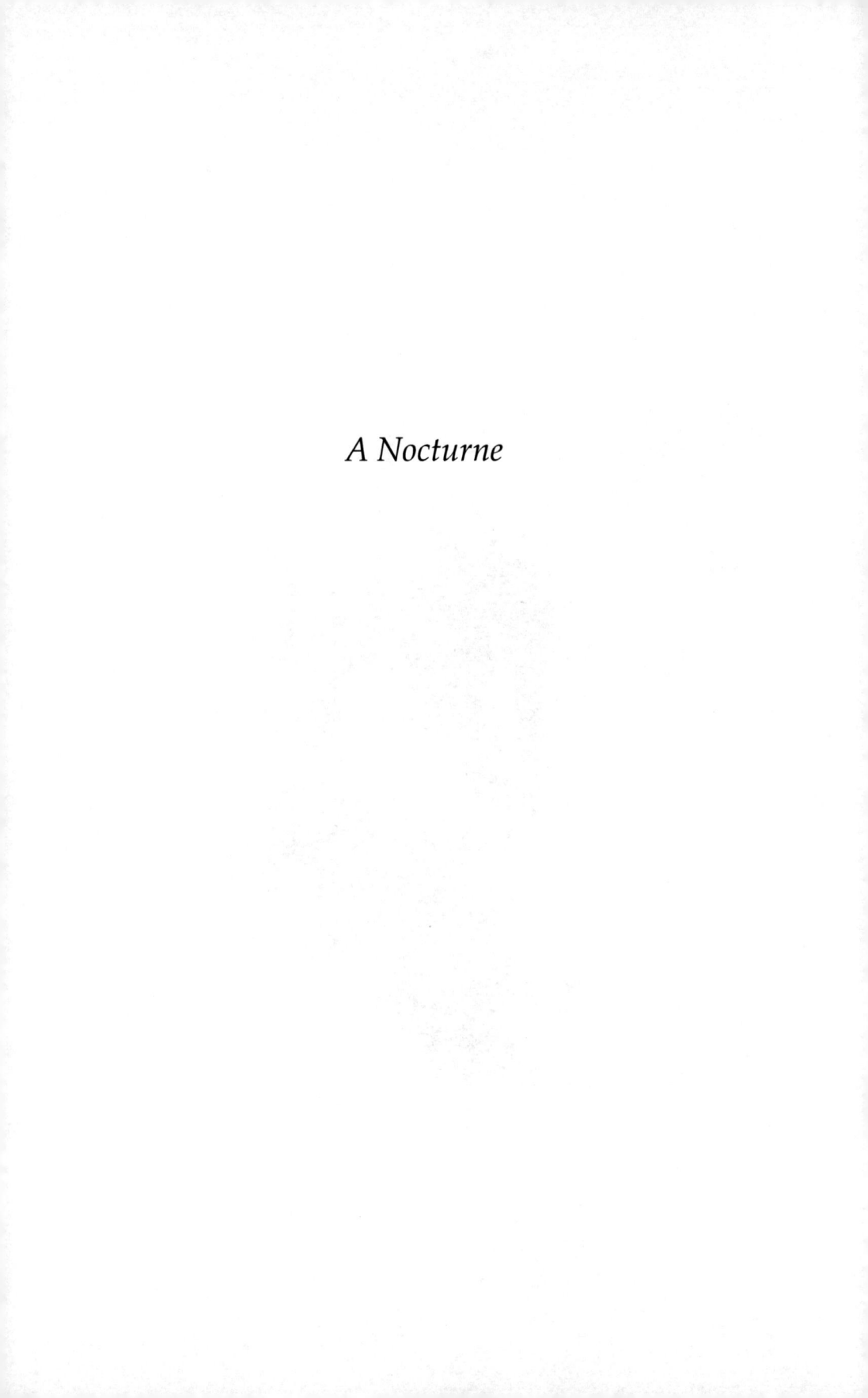

A Nocturne

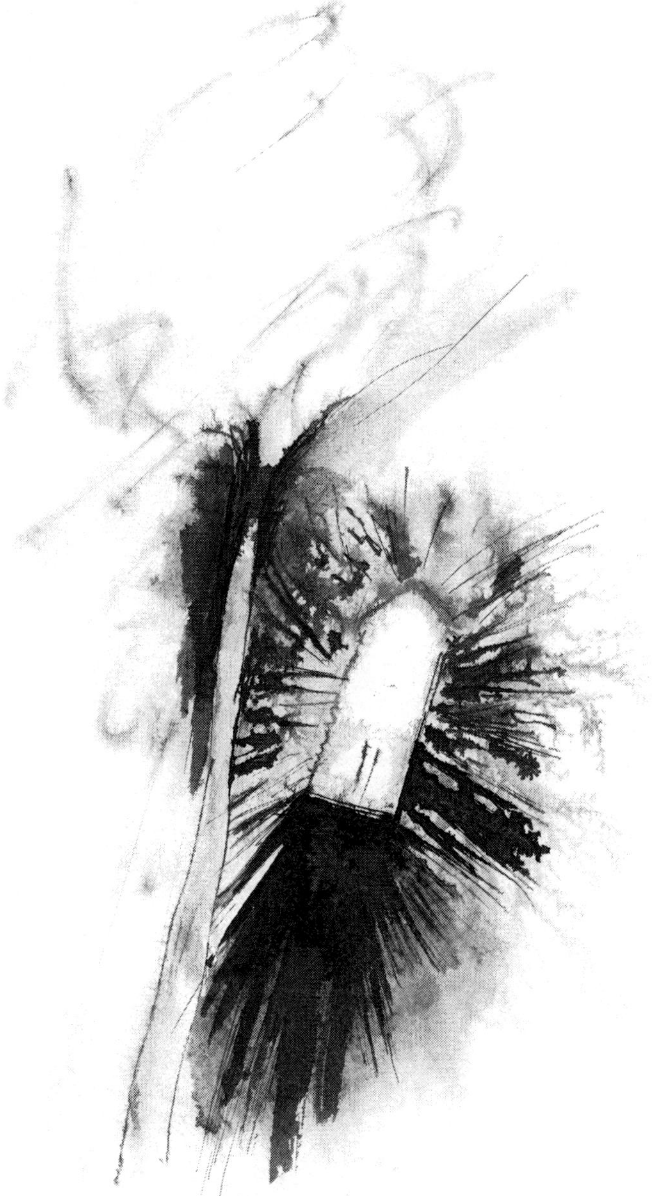

A NOCTURNE

It was night again, in late August. Albeit a night
on which the moon did not dance along geometry's chalked line,
and the stars, with their falling Lyrids, did not tear up eternity's telegrams –
not before nor after reading them …
The Earth's spirits had organized a run with extinguished torches …
The darkness – without the illuminating background of deer eyes
and therefore so absolute that it always misses
the beginning of every kill and the end of every murder –
overtook me on that day, high up in the hills.
But, it was heath I smelled and a fleeting irritation of air by fog,
when a gypsy moth with a golden anus flew past;
but, I also smelled a gallant fear, as hairy as Hector,
emanating from my entire body
as my fantasy's idolatry incinerated within itself
a mysterious rustling, almost a crackling, of one nullity after another …
Somewhat deeper I sensed the presence of a grove and a ravine
through which, as the unfolding sound eluded to, perhaps a rivulet flowed
with a covered bridge at one end …

Falling with half my soul's memories as they spilled over my cerebral weir
into my childhood, a time so easily betrayed,
I thought of those whom I had once harmed,
and as I gazed down below, I was filled with a melancholy that
could not summon a single way of blushing for all those black times.

But, how much I also yearned to touch
a certain letter inside my breast pocket – a gripping letter,
its script like an eagle's beak attached to a dove's neck –
and this precisely now, during the Easter week of self-denial, when lust
so excellently illuminates the portrait of one's beloved! …

He who drinks wine rings big bells. But women
do not love drunkards … "Do we fall so short for you as that?"
they ask and then grind us down by, for instance, counting items of laundry
and, now and again, brooding over their maiden monogram
or by ruining our vinaceous blood,
and (since at times there can be too much intention in a form,
so that nothing else can fit into it)
they round out and aerate their empty beauty
with the yeast of anger …

VLADIMÍR HOLAN

I thought of that just now, as I looked downwards –
with my self-hatred accumulating at such a crinkly speed that its snake scales
could have smothered anything –
when (and what sense is there in one's autobiography)
a lantern appeared in that valley below ...

The lantern appeared so suddenly and so without warning
that I wouldn't have recognized my own silence,
had I been forced to speak,
and I would have spurned my obsessive feelings,
which well know that all the words' meanings are God's ...
It appeared so suddenly and I, who had just recently been stretched
on the torture rack of my qualms,
was now allowed, spellbound, to participate in
the motion of a heart's moveable feast.
If it first appeared below in the darkness
and then near the alders, it was now already near the aspens –
and if I had known the shrub near where it found itself next,
I wouldn't have hesitated to ceremoniously name it,
and if I had known its name,
I would have tortured myself covetously with the yearning
to know how to utter it ... Indeed, it is true
that our love is lessened by our wounded language ...

The lantern's motion, free and not subordinated,
lived in its little flame, and in that flame
everything was all as one, just as everything was all as one in our mother,
with the abundant assurance
that All Saints' day could have already come and gone,
and yet you would still be only warming yourself up ...

In that little flame everything existed all at once,
just as everything exists all at once in poverty,
which must not even ask
whether something else still remained, but
which could, in the end, offer
the entire world at a feast for the poor ...
In that little flame everything existed all at once,
just as life exists all at once and so do the dead,
the repudiated dead who, it is said,

A NOCTURNE

cannot reveal themselves to us who are still living,
but who do reveal themselves to us ...
In that little flame both the candle and the oil burned for them;
a glowing heat burned for them there ...
In that little flame the grapes had already ripened long ago,
as a heroic minimum for a poet
who already existed long ago, and who would only later go mad ...
In that little flame was both the joy of the senses,
as well as the sorrow of the soul, and the knowledge
that it all would soon reverse itself ...
In that little flame was the never-ending patience
of human tribulation ... I was not therefore alone ...

Meanwhile, the lantern had advanced almost to the centre of the valley.
Its left beam was like an upended tin of turpentine,
and its luminosity reminded me more abruptly
of that letter inside my breast pocket, and also of a certain hall
into which, years ago – without getting stuck in too many details –
swing had intruded, straight from the loutish jazz years, and now,
with its face like thunder, it glared with an eagle's eye.
The hall was filled with smoke ... La vida es sueño ...
I felt myself being guarded and wanted to find out by whom ...
But, there was no God there, merely an essence without an existence,
and there is no difference whether temptation
is entered or fallen into ... We are a desert,
which we hold in our fist, but it just keeps changing into dust ...

A single grain of that dust seemed like a rock to me then –
as in "a female rock consents softly" ...
Without any ribald motives to ingratiate myself to the vibraphone,
I approached her ... We fell in love.
We talked and, enraptured, we awkwardly inhabited
the singularity of words, but solely the heritable ones.
But we knew how sometimes not to reply,
and later we danced and drank wine and ate bread,
without needing to use the crumbs to wipe off
the gouache of soot and tears ... And ill-advised was anyone
who dared to imagine her underbelly's hair
being harvested on that very night,
just because the grass on Carmen's grave had turned ruddy by then,

and that a mute woman would chop down a tree on that very night,
and a blind man would not jump aside,
and that the result would be an offspring of jealousy,
who too soon outgrows the lovers and
grows even as far as murder and execution,
just as a dagger and sword are really nothing more than extended
    fingernails ...
El mayor monstruo los cellos ... But no,
we stepped out into the street and nobody even dared
to offer us, on the black market of realism,
Beethoven's earpiece ... We were a dream
without the three-fold star of adultery ... And
what sense is there then in one's autobiography
with its displeasing leniency towards an eggshell
and its fearfulness of a funeral urn! ...

All this I contemplated atop that hill,
no longer feeling like myself ...
An emotional renewal – a tragic renewal, I was telling myself.
It is better not to be, I was telling myself. Better to be a dead man
than a living fucker, I was telling myself.
Better to be a non-phallus and a non-fuck than Uriah's letter, I was telling
    myself.
Better to be a devil who believes – even if it is a belief without love –
than to be us, we who love but do not believe, I was telling myself.
Better to be a dead poet than he who sings Christmas carols
and who therefore only begs, begs from people who are
held together by tenacious bovine ligaments,
I was telling myself. And, it is not necessary to search for a desert grave,
in order to die in the mountains, I was telling myself,
and I gazed again down towards the valley
where the lantern had already receded, faded away and then vanished ...

Blackness tolerates only verdure ... And so,
not until later, when dawn had begun working
its cold needle into copper, I pondered
who might have carried that light ... A disguise was ruled out ...
Therefore, only a priest could have carried it then;
a priest walking with the Lord
or a virgin ... Therefore, not a dona Cruente

A NOCTURNE

or a Clare Junonie, their theatre having been closed by the plague,
but the one who as a saintess had
already in her childhood yearned not to thrive but to wane ...

(1950)

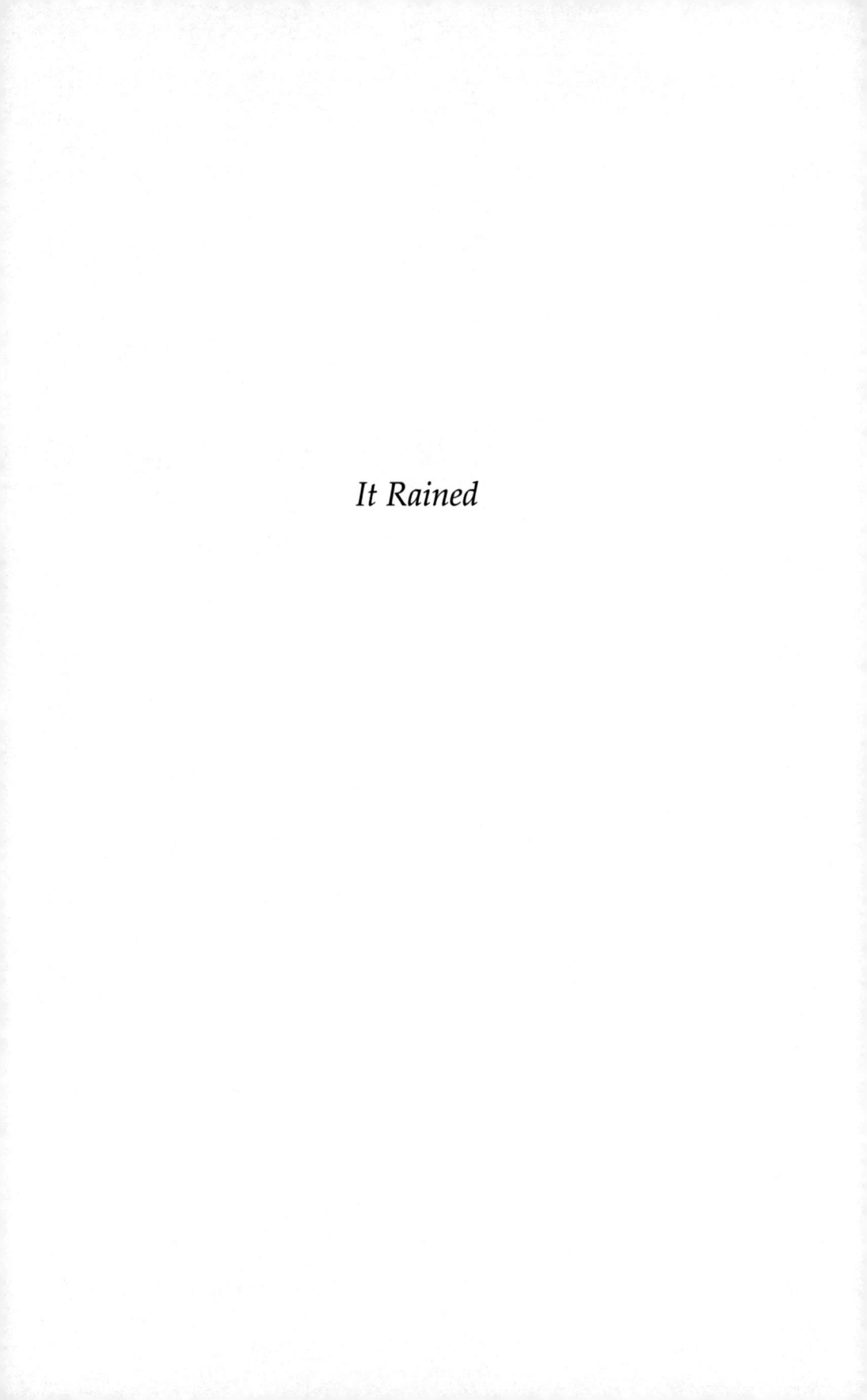

It Rained

IT RAINED

When it rains, they say a drunkard is dying,
and the rooster won't sing because he abhors the rain …

It rained … The sunlight, retracted by the park's left side,
was reposing on the subjective green.
Music in a wet entr'acte,
converted inch by inch into soliloquy,
dared to invite its opponent …
And he did not waver between stepping out from a funereal procession of
    moments
and taking a seat by an open fire
where Venus Vulgivaga, that mother of blind love,
half-closed his and my eyelids
and opened a spoken testament …

VLADIMÍR HOLAN

I

It isn't true! I said ... But he said: It is!
After all, if love is vigilant,
then the lovers' aloofness will appear undisguised ... I knew them both ...
It's not without dread that I tell you they loved each other
and were used to each other, and their wedding day was approaching,
with a nine-tier wedding cake on a plate
and meat dangling in the parson's chimney ...
One day they had arranged
that on the following Sunday they would go to the Saint's day fair,
each of them to a different village ... And that they would meet
at midnight near the marlstone quarry ...

And they met: she – dressed in twenty petticoats –
she was, to this day, well versed in reading musical scores
so that, with her ball mask accreted to her face,
she no longer feared snakes ...
And he – with a few gulps of brandy
to give him a handsel from Salomon's bottle –
he, a lanky fellow, used to lean his ladder against the world
and perhaps even waved his finger at fate who wore leaden boots
(because there is always one child whom the mother favours most!).
One can still see, from the lascivious etching on the moon,
how they kissed each other
and embraced each other in the least creaky of nature's door frames,
and (although man is perishing, to date only the horse and the bee
are dying) they were almost ready to hit the bull's eye –
when they realized suddenly
that neither one of them had brought for the other a present from the fair ...

And, as if in one stroke, they found their true names,
but did not yet know how to pronounce them;
at first, they felt ashamed of their silence,
but then, close to tears, they stopped gazing into each other's eyes,
and later, filled with pity and anger, they let their tears go
so that they could blindly reproach each other
about there being nothing left of the other, not even a dream –
for nothing had been left, not even by their ancestors –
and that they, in fact, cannot entrust each other with anything,

IT RAINED

and that they should therefore part the way fire rises
and water falls ... Each of them, one lonely half!
And part they did ... They still wrote to each other
but threw the unopened letters into the fire,
and the letters hissed like hog's bile
thrown onto cinder ... Never again did they catch sight of each other ...

Is the first stone in a quarry the same as the second one?

II

It isn't true! he said. But I said: It is!
After all, every month has an unlucky day ...
I once stood close to the moor
and contemplated an abandoned brick yard ...
It too, like the adjacent cottage,
had long ago dropped from the executioner's hand
into extinction ... The shallow trench around it
only served to emphasize the walls and caved-in roof.
But in one wall the windows and a door still survived.
And this door, as I was gazing at it,
suddenly opened and a woman appeared,
a woman so beautiful
that I felt offended, astonished, joyful or crazy ...

I'm in favour of foolishness; I was astounded and therefore was not ashamed
    of my silence ...
Even if I had arrived on the very last night train
and then, on foot, had outrun the sunrise,
I would have missed the daybreak ... Even if I had eaten
bile from a fish, I would not have healed my blindness.
Even if I had offered both banks to a river,
I would not have discovered the spring.
Even if I had adored her,
I would not have been allowed to recognize her,
not even by her convincing gait ...

It is true that she too only *stood* there and looked around,
and when she noticed the storks flying towards the mountains,
she stepped back inside again
and closed the door behind her ...

And where I had just been astounded, I was already desirous
and thus was jealous, and I felt as though I had to transform
that door of her vanished beauty into the window of a madhouse
from which I would be allowed to pine freely
for three kinds of worlds – I turned to bravery,
rushed recklessly towards the door, opened it
and searched behind it ...

IT RAINED

But, I found no one ...

Only the dust in that place could have perhaps given shape
to the statue of the sculptor, who would have recreated her image.
Only a chimera might have perhaps admitted the poet
who, only after forgetting himself, would have been summoned by a dream
to substantiate her appearance ...
But, only Jesus Christ would have perhaps had
Pontius Pilate's wife painted there ...
Perhaps ... But, who can know? ...

Who does know? Perhaps, in truth, purity only exists in the desert ...

(1950)

Susannah in the Bath

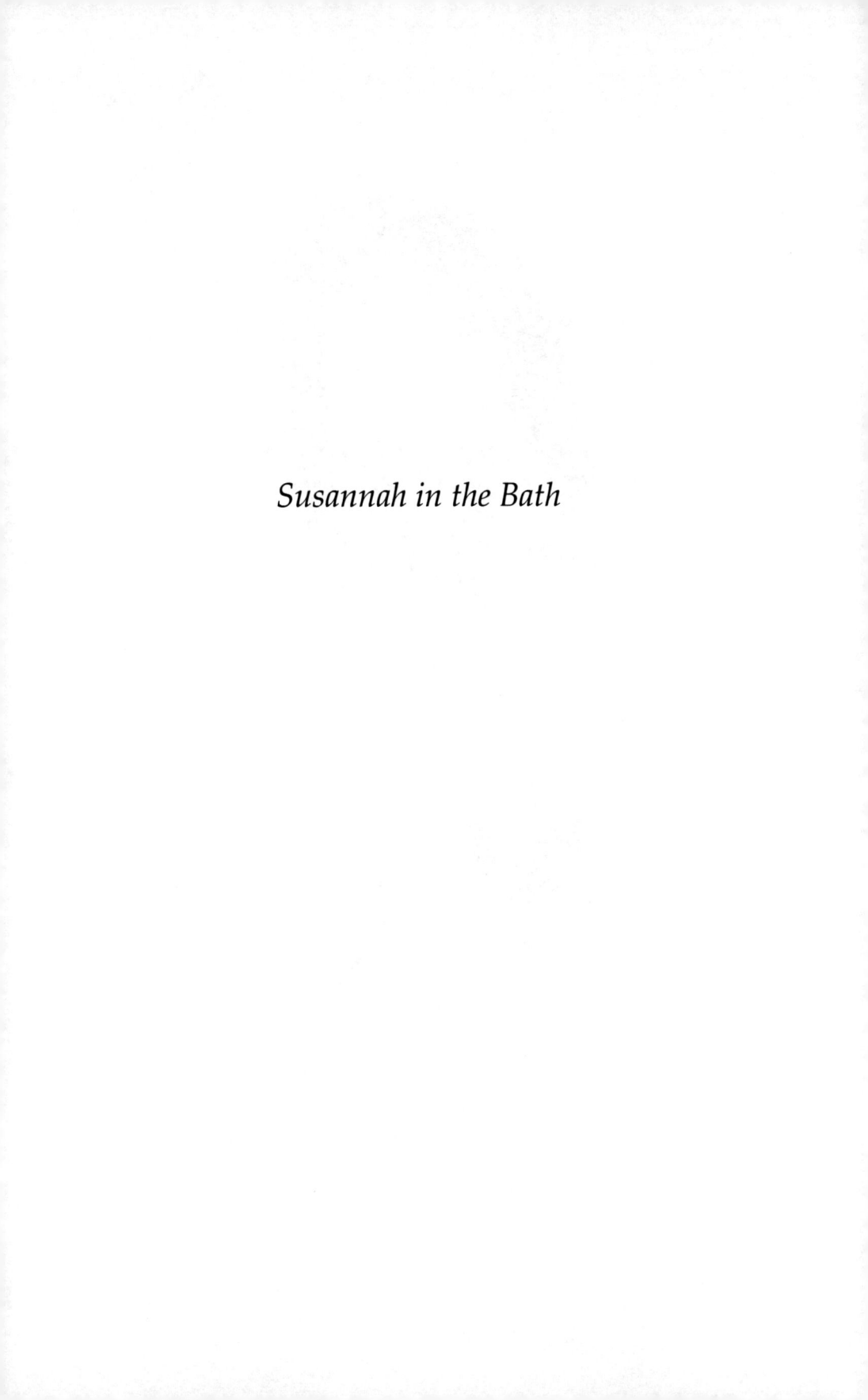

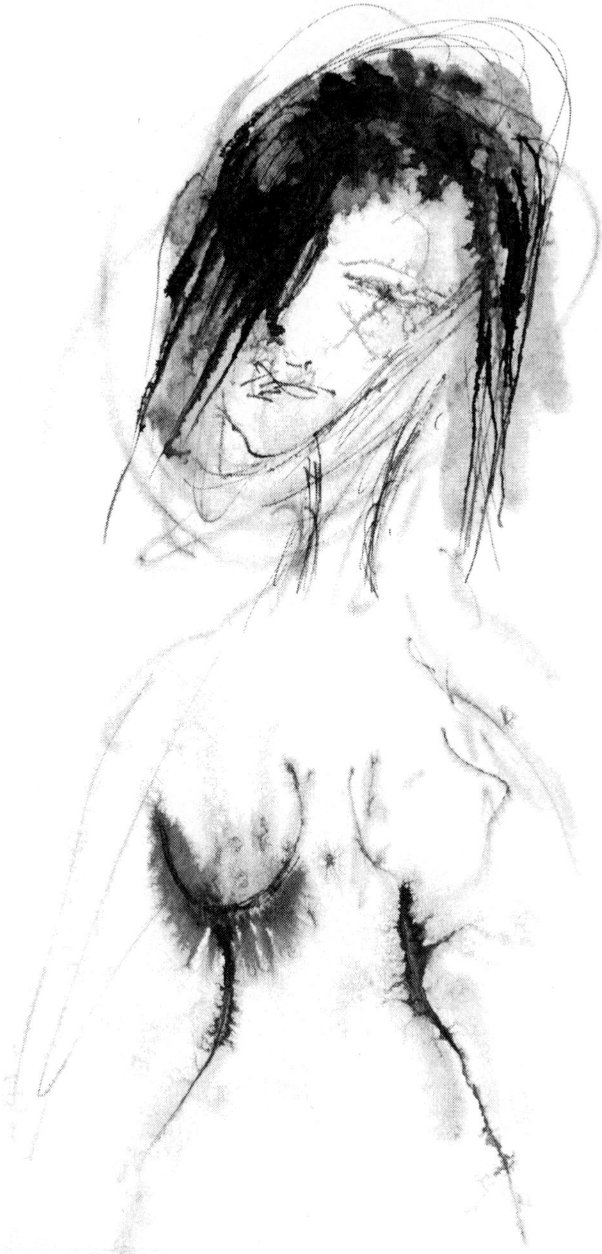

SUSANNAH IN THE BATH

One year had passed ... And yet, in despair it isn't life that is at stake, but
 existence.
It was solely the death of my most precious sister that reminded me
how I still loved. Though it was a despairing love, one
that almost consented to suicide,
it was a love that still partook in the mysteries
and thus faced nothingness.

Invited by no one, I lived
in the tiny turret of a fort built to a square plan
with an adjacent dilapidated fold yard and forge shop.
The turret had just two levels,
but if perchance someone were to fall from there,
for three days he would be unable to speak and would be given saltwater to
 drink.
The turret was long-lived: its last landlord,
Kaprynal Tluxa, liber baro a Kunovitz,
had lived there a century ago. He was assassinated,
like Saint Gleb, by his own cook.

Carried away by Satan on the hipbone of dumbness, I was there on the
 lookout
for just over half a year waiting for an illumination
without deeds and thus boundless.
The countryside wasn't harsh: there were groves, though of the soaring kind;
there were clouds, though of the pedestrian kind.
And occasionally the pauses in the nightingale's song were so majestic
that they commanded temporality's ecclesiastical tongue –
and sometimes the nearby bog, just like a "primus" stove,
scattered will-o'-the-wisps and broiled mosquito lard over them ...
Few steps further was a rise, where White Beam, Turkish Oak, Honey
 Suckle
and especially Forest Oak dunked their hands, like wrestlers of old, into
 tannin
to stop them from slipping.

Those oaks held together the district road
along which, regularly at around eleven in the morning,
the baker's horse, by the name of Skinsack, jingled along in its harness.
Those oaks held together even the distant narrow-gauge train,

whose whistle urged the selfsame horse to urinate.
The cricket's neighbourhood was entirely made of thread.
While the children instinctively gathered cumin in the meadows
(carum carvi!) … From the golden remoteness of hope,
bells rang up to the clouds; the footnotes of villages
beneath the horizon's line sometimes led me
across the moor into the distance where I found
a Dog's Foot Violet, which was then already rare in our region.
And during a rainfall, which had been plucked while it was still green,
the vesper bell wilted in an affiliated church,
where as if the ribs had squeezed the egg of the vault
and had thrown the yolk behind the head of a Saint.
The chaplain of that church I met later.
He was poor: his chimney wasn't redolent with ham,
and he even had to ring the bells himself. He believed that at the Last
    Judgment
the bad would rise with their bodies and the good without them.
Once, we talked about the lost paradise.
He surmised that on the first night after the fall the devil slept with Eve,
on the second night an angel, and on the third night Adam.
The devil slept with her because of his pride, the angel because of his pity
    and Adam
because he was jealous, while she was curious about disillusionment …
He was an admirable priest and, unless I forget, I will tell you more about
    him.

But, let me come back: beneath that little turret was a cellar.
When you opened the door, the entrance, from the top to halfway down,
was nailed shut with a thick metal plate … You recalled
a certain dungeon in Paris that was just the same,
though for the sole purpose of forcing the queen and the poet, both
    condemned,
to bow their head down to their waist upon entering.
That this place had once also been a prison, I recognised
from the outlines of the female genitalia carved into the plaster.

On the first floor dwelled a farrago of junk: a downfallen coat of arms and
    realism.
On the second floor lived I … The kerosene tongue ceaselessly
licked there at Pascal's fly, St. Augustine's aching teeth

SUSANNAH IN THE BATH

and several other books, all in the same binding
because I don't like women who change into a new dress
to greet their guests ... At another time, the tongue of that lamp,
like a spike thrust by the fire into the flame, speared
my camp bed and cloak, my suitcase filled with linen and a little food,
so as to avoid anything that does not fit into an eye.
But, that which doesn't fit into an eye, is not the same as that which doesn't enter there
where one cannot see ... Nevertheless, even the silence coarsened;
it was insolent and talked back to me, and the cricket, too,
called: suffer, suffer, suffer! – How it all reverberated therein,
and how rightly a friend of mine,
who had once visited me there, named my week
the cavern of seven corners: Heptymachos! ... Enough of that!

My petty food purchases were supplied by a certain old woman
from the village ... One day, when I saw her approaching,
it occurred to me that according to our roads,
the earth's door resides in woman,
but according to our footsteps, death is already inside the house ...
At that time she brought me several eggs ... I clapped shut
a just-read book, in which the Orfics toyed
with their bracket fungi, and I asked her
whether she feared death and believed in resurrection
and eternal life ... I beheld a snub-nosed surprise
on her face; it was somewhat theatrical considering
how quickly it changed into distemper ... And she was as if transformed
into a harridan who'd drunk some vixen's milk,
so cunning was her reticence! –

I fear scoffers before they've made up their mind ...
Perhaps she was just remembering,
but I sensed
that her soul's memory was merely nervous.
The door of her gaze creaked with the dryness of her eye.
When she guessed that I, myself, am floundering in creed against creed,
she lowered her eyes and then a boiling over, a kind of fury,
scribbled in blue onto her lids like onto a film of boiling milk ...
In the same way a blind man met a wood dryad ... Then she said,
but she said it as if to suggest

that not even things could remain silent about certain testimonies,
because time condemns their creator:
"If we didn't want to abandon life, we'd be
shut inside it ... We live into worries and then we start dying ...
To die is to make the graveyard humpbacked ...
Wooden houses are already crumbling in the woods ...
And after death? ... Nothing of the kind! ... You cut a cockerel's throat,
the blood flows out and then nothing is left, not even a goose egg! ...
The pulpiter in his sermons is lying ..." – I don't know how,
but suddenly, and no farther than three cubits from me,
there appeared, non-figuratively, a certain philosopher,
with the wood shavings of his eyebrows retracted by the magnet of his
    reflection:
Post mortem nihil est, ipsaque mors nihil ...

At first, I was alarmed, for I feared the night within me,
which would have alienated the trustfulness of any child ...
Then I realized, but this also only on a child's fare,
that I was well acquainted with being shaken out by nothingness
like a straw bed on which the taciturn poet lies,
and that if no one threatens us, then we remain nobodies
in a wilderness that is hauled along by the agitation of boulders
that must spread out ... And yet,
when platitude blooms, a miracle has already sprouted ...
Only limbo lasts longer than mercy, which sometimes is
ignited by a blackout: and suddenly, I pitied the old woman.
Perhaps my compassion, in contrast to her black-bile certainty
without a skerrick of irony, tasted sentimental to me;
perhaps I whispered to myself: what can sympathy do,
being too powerless to speak a single word?
It will even muffle our heartbeat
and turn it into a mere presence ... Yes, but that presence
was here: pallomenén kardián – the still-beating heart ...

Whereas most human beings accept the tidings about the unchangeability
of this or that colour as though perceived through an opal,
with this old woman one couldn't even willow a diamond.
Hardened, she suddenly said: "A butcherbird feels death ...
I know my coffin and yet don't know my down payment ..."

Through what body could one illuminate such traces of the spirit?
Is it possible, I asked myself, that I am witness
to everything that my soul possesses, which it hands out, even throws out,
but which my blood has not accepted? ... "It is cold in here!"
she said. "Willy-nilly they used to put on fox-fur coats
in chambers such as these! ... And you're in need of some wine!" she added,
as if she felt sorry for me, and I whispered dumbly to myself:
Behold the mother! and I gazed at her
out of the firmest place in my tears ... She, however,
rushed in with a scornful reminder:
"You know, my mother used to shout at me: 'Look here,
the way you got soaked again, you'll get a drunkard for a husband!' –
And I got one ..." She mumbled the end of that sentence
almost wintrily and became silent, as if it were imperative to wait
for her inner lake to freeze over. Or else, the heaviest of her recollections
would never cross to the other bank ...

Later, I acquainted myself with the local gravedigger, Mezoun.
I don't know whether he was playing the fool,
staring as if he had water in his head,
but after all he did live merely off godmother brandy ...
"Alcohol," he claimed, "is a mirror in which one can see the entire world."
He was not dumb. Where I expected a nymph to suddenly step out
of a tree, he immediately knew that oakwood shavings
purified wine, that pearwood cured ham,
that alderwood made good paving blocks in the horse stable,
and that a certain kind of young hazel tree had to be transplanted higher and higher,
and underlain with little stones, so that its roots wouldn't grow too deep ...

He meant no harm but had unlucky hands, and what the sun had shown him
was brought to him by the moon ... He constantly insisted that he would die soon
and that already he was peering into the parson's purse: "But because I'll die
in rather good health, I fear falling ill after my death," he awkwardly used to add.
They said about him that at one time he deserted his studies ... It was he himself,
all bone and nose, who visited me one rainy day.

Rinsing down the ham with a brandy he'd named "trouble"
and, in truth, not caring about the cyclic nature of the world,
he could have concentrated on the tragic dance
and like a black artist could have invoked out of his greyest epoch
the story of Dora Závětová ... But, he simply said:
"Right now, when fatigue has become a luxury,
even flies can't stand the colour blue ... It's just vanity, sir;
I know people well! ... How much of anything they'll throw under a hearse
to slow it down ... And how much of anything they'll level in front of it
to speed it up ... But, should you be curious about Závětová
(*who comes to you* nowadays doused
in the most acrid vinegar), she used to be a real beauty –
that's a good fifty years back now –
and since then a large rock's been pressing upon my heart!"

After a deliberate pause, he tried to persuade me rather crazily
that once, on a certain embankment, he had not been the third spectator
concealed in a decayed weeping willow, and that he never
had been in love with Dora ...

"I don't understand you!" I said. "That doesn't matter!" he riposted with self-
    satisfaction
and then went on: "Dora? A great beauty she certainly was! You could have
    recognized her
by her very gait! " ... A real beauty! ... But man gladly offers the habitual
to his fright or else to his enchantment. Man!
He had only just become great but was already mediocre ...
Her beauty was so down-to-earth that we couldn't see her anymore.
A virgin! God's masterpiece, wherein fate, with its melodious accidentality,
was merely an apprentice ... A virgin and an only child ...
Can you see, beyond the upper end of the moor,
there where a field lies fallow, that building?
That is where she was born; it is the mill Litterdust ..."
_ _

One day, Dora went to bathe in a nearby pond ...
It was towards evening ... The seam-side of the meadow nuzzled itself
    against the pine needles,
and this splendour concentrated the sultriness into such an after-taste
that it was through music that vertigo's trumpet expressed the cuprous

sensations ...
You could also compare it to the oily reek a mechanic carries on him,
or a bin filled with flour that has gone rancid
and is, perhaps, opened by a hungry orphan ...

But before long, the formlessness
of this slumber, of this trance,
in which we often talk to ourselves, was transformed ...
The only colours: black and green weren't allowed to mix ...
It was forbidden to kill snakes ... Nature
suddenly became ceremonial ... But that ceremony
concealed a bossiness, which was ready at anytime to burst forth ...

Dora knew and chose that bathing place
because of its gloomy expanse; it was congruous with her emotional rhythm
and could interpret itself to her as a kind of Balladia.
But it was her shoes, made of red sheepskin
and carefully placed under a willow,
that talked about Romancia, who, naked,
stood up to her waist in water, as if she had stopped
at the steps of beauty leading into the mirror ... Two strings of pearls
guarded, like cromlechs, the mounds
of her not-yet-kissed breasts ... Her plaits had, perhaps, been smoothed
with a comb made of goldfish bonelets and straightened with a brush
made of good-luck pennies ... If she painted her eyebrows,
then it was only with a match burnt in the flame of poesy ...
The dark dint of her navel was merely snow, which had melted
beneath her twin's finger ... Her hips and buttocks
had something golden about them, which could only be understood
by disastrous men ... The water's surface, torn by the caressing of a wave
as it moved up to the hock of her Venus' vein, presaged
the woman within the virgin ... Ah, the devil
has enough sugar! Even there, where the sugar itself is black! ...

In idolatry: the encroaching desire expects
reverberant renunciation and a levitating goddess.
The one here was a goddess without sanctity.
To worship one like her means not to utter blasphemies,
but only if you are a heathen ...

VLADIMÍR HOLAN

The water burned inextinguishably around her and
matched her beauty, which was, like a phantasm,
eternal in its sensual incorporeality and summoned lust
to become more mortal ...

Hadn't two juvenile upstarts been observing her
for a goodly time already? ... They had come to water their horses and now,
concealed in the hedges, were looking through a leafy peephole
(a Judas' eye – that little window in a prison cell
through which prisoners are spied upon).
Blinded at first, they dripped chimerical water into their eyes
so that they could behold everything – and then they sipped perceptibly
from their poppy-red breath, while their spinal cord
blissfully swallowed the crushed-glass sensation of a frisson ...
Forced singing at the wine harvest protects the grapes,
but they remained silent ...

Because their lasciviousness was impatient,
nothing hindered them ... They wanted, they did not yearn ...
They should have gone mad but were only crazed
as they tumbled from the first floor of semblances ...
What then can be done about such anaemic delays,
which had been thrown,
long before, into dragons' heads for consideration!
Opportunity only takes notice of those who are cunning! ... Why then
should they have to wait for their silver to be stamped into coinage?
Why should they exert themselves by pulling the rings
off the swollen fingers of their recklessness? Why not dare
and plunge from a creative limbo into a ravishing
world without witnesses?

It was getting dark ... Dogs were drying their teeth in the moonlight ...
With each passing wave, the holes along the shoreline churned
the magisterium, that masterful dust made from crayfish eyes ...
Sounds strolled among all the feminine names ...

Those two, meanwhile, didn't need
to squint at the sun or begrudge
what they themselves had placed in its way: their shadows ... Both of them,
were (with the exception of the gash on a touchstone)

SUSANNAH IN THE BATH

not ignorant of the gash in the barley, the gash on the beer coaster
or the gash in a woman; both of them now moved furtively ahead
under a semi-cruciform structure of passion without man –
while the girl, not surprised by the two beasts before her,
admitted abruptly that since one already lies so much about reality,
she could trifle with it a little more ... To trifle with it here,
or along the Ionic coast or somewhere in the valley of Quito! ...
She almost threw herself into that play.
She was on the verge of placing a wager,
had she remained with the two of them
most alone, all of herself:
for adventure does not know the central force of disharmony ...

Yet, we tend to be incomprehensibly precise
as we flee from ourselves ...
But something happened, something intimate within her,
and it was therefore not in a foreign language
that her life's existence was denied.

Thereupon, every single moment became impossible ...

But she did not want to blame it on eternity ...
If lightning had struck a shepherd's staff,
it would have shown how many beasts keep an eye on an inhabited dream,
and how the being parts from the creature ...
She conceded to fate's approval,
but only in its neglected darkness –
and she surrendered herself to both youths,
being thoroughly autumnal beneath her own vernal cloud;
yes, thoroughly autumnal like the star Fomalhaud ...

_____

Everything is questioned just there where we love ...
But she did not love ... Even if she understood
ere she desired, afterwards she ceased looking
through the hole in her Sunday dress at Monday's bare-naked nail ...
Sensing that irony is above satire, just as private life is contrary to public life,
she did not seek to cover her shame with floss silk ...
And, ravished, she did not sew voluminous sleeves out of crimson taffeta
so as to stow slander there ...

VLADIMÍR HOLAN

It went from bad to worse for her:
people coughed as she entered the church …
They whispered in hushed tones behind her back whenever she entered
 a shop …
They wrote anonymous letters to the dean, telling him to use the strap
braided from the beard of Moses …
Even outside in the fields she was indistinct,
because she was chaste, and she changed almost everyone's
scenery into a landscape with a pubic cottage
where they could shout at her to let herself go in an anus dance …

Life leaves nothing to spare in an orphan's book.
Affluence tends to be more tight-fisted … Her parents,
who still weighed everything in pounds and kvintels,
hardened their hearts when she refused
to name her "seducer" – and they betrothed her
to a non-resident cobbler on the Monday before Candlemas.
Because they were mealy-mouthed,
they provided no more than half a hair
for the satirical sequel that was her wedding …

Thereupon, to knock perchance on their door
meant one would hear: "Mind your own business, you archdoublewhore
weaned on viperous milk!"
To tap perchance on their window meant one would hear:
"Oh, go piss up a rope!"
She attempted it later under the cover of darkness, but only the hollow moon,
the pittance-moon, tossed her a white Groschen for a black day …

But by then her belly was already growing and people called her names …
And, since a written word is better than a spoken one,
they closed the book of maledictum so that one day,
on the wall of the hemp kiln and then on the wall of the morgue,
she would encounter her name followed by an exclamation mark,
which, though just a concept and yet already a commentary,
even forced itself onto the hour-distant
city ramparts … You could read there in stalactic tar:
such and such a strumpet … And this pillory-stake footnote:
Dorothy – stinky soap!

SUSANNAH IN THE BATH

At one time that girl used to read ... But long ago
she stopped singing. Long ago the blank verse,
bent to a golden arc by the urinating Apollo,
extinguished in her what may have merely been the cinders
of a vehement hankering for the truth and, thus, for the impossible ...
And even if it were true that the poems
she once used to read were about renewal rather
than about resuscitation, and not even about the perception of things
but about their subversion during the hedgehog's reign –
those verses were on a perpetual holiday, while the hedgehog had to toil.

By now she should have known him, the cobbler and the jealous man,
the roughneck and the ruffian, who, after his daily return
from Gin Lane, used to shout at her:
"Wherefore *the wheel* of fate? I can't see any meaning in it!"
And when she (unwisely, if you like, because by that time she no longer
showed a noble mien but her true character traits, indeed, just one single trait
– so long as stubbornness can have more of them than a unicorn),
and when she reasoned with him: " Just turn the light on!" –
he shouted: "You think I can reach it?!"
And then he let the cudgel dance along her back, beating it
black and blue, not slackening until she had begun to turn four-legged,
being only sated after she fell and losing his consciousness after arriving
in Phallustown, where even the devil refused to do any devilry
precisely because of that unconsciousness ...

Gravid with child, coarsened, upturned and pensive,
she gave birth soon after the wedding. From her infant's tear,
even she learned where the sea was the saltiest ...
The cobbler Achatius was at that very moment savouring a pork uterus.
He had insisted on a girl. When they told him that it was a boy,
he spat out the meat and left for the tavern. After barely a year,
he began to wallop the child, so much more so since Dora was not one
to give life and then refuse to protect it ...

_ _

"Once," – continued the grave digger – "once, I paid them a visit
before Christmas. The little boy may have been approaching his fifth year ...
He ran up to me and said: 'Uncle, does the Christ Child have a bum?'
'Why do you ask?' say I ... And the boy went on: 'Well,

because father said the Christ Child would give me diddly-shit!' "

Some alcohol is so strong, the bottom of the glass flies off.
The grave digger fell silent and glared with a scowl
as the last gulp of gin disappeared ...
Its disappearance was a hint for him to get up and leave,
to leave and light a lantern in the crypt
of squire Kaptynal. "I've got to go," he said,
"it's his birthday tomorrow, but remember this, sir:
Eve is life and Adam is a man of the earth;
as it leaps, so it bows, but one day
the earth will cease to be a bowstring!"
This, I said, you must have read somewhere!
"Sir," he said, "crypt or no crypt, what are we
besides our wages and daily bread? Eternal damnation indeed:
the earth opens and then closes!"

I saw him off down the stairs because he was staggering.
"What?!" he said, "I've been drinking for a good forty years,
but I happen to be an invalid and that's why I waddle ...
You see, I once cracked my collarbone ...
But, they gave me the wrong treatment ... Not before that little bone pierced
    a masseur
did they rush me for an X-ray ... Little bone ... Bone ...
It was quite so (he mumbled) in those days, in those days
a piece of meat without a bone perforated a virgin ..."

What about the other two? I asked him abruptly,
as he took a breather downstairs under a corbel ...

He stiffened ... Not in dreamy melancholy
but in a sullen, squinting distrust.
"Them?" he said not with his own mouth ... "You know, they're like
two pelts from a single ox ... Oldrich walked into his joiner's knife,
and a funeral knoll came out of it ... *And the third one*
(and here he began to chuckle), *the third one*, I swear
I wouldn't bet my bottom dollar that he's still alive ...
Thrice he tried it on a beam in the belfry,
and thrice he was prevented from drowning
in the hangman's hemp ... What then is one to do but waddle

SUSANNAH IN THE BATH

along with muddy vengeance ... You know, I once read
that life isn't only how we live,
for we are lived by life too ... Blast it! ...
No, this doesn't mean I have any misgivings, no, far from it;
but I can't forget, you know, *forget*
one particular night, which followed that "bathing".
Barely had I led the horses into the stable,
when, oh boy, what a thunderstorm burst forth!
Thunderclaps were serving each other
devil's excrement, smack-bang across our fence ...
At the landlords', they were still burning candles for their departed Sweet-
    tooth
with retracted wicks in order to scrimp, you understand ...
How soundlessly I behaved in the midst of that insane roar
from the heavens! ... I held my breath,
took off my boots and climbed up the ladder into the hay.
Then a rainstorm erupted: no thought of sleeping,
and until the cock crowed I heard the rain in the yard
filling up my gumboots ... As a matter of fact sir, yes,
you should leave here soon ..." –
he added a while later, not so much as a threat
but as a kind of dismal regard
to ingratiate himself with his own frightfulness ...
Since he hadn't scared me, he opened his mouth
in which only few tusks remained,
but he opened it as if untying
a bag filled with chunks of arsenic ... And he said:
"You know, it's not at all unsympathetic where we are now!" – – –

I like tower Jackdaws ... The old woman flushed them out several times
after the grave digger's talk. ... The last time
(and it was just as it had been recorded in the old annals:
the rain dripped with blood and snow fell overnight upon the rain),
she brought me hog's pudding soup ... I clapped shut
the Book of Pyramids, where I had just read
that during the time of Ptolemy II a certain participant
in the festivities of Adonis bought from the priests
for one drachma sausages made from sacrificial beasts ...

As I looked out the window at the barberry tree growing out of the fence,

I asked her about the name of the brook
that drove the mill in which she had been born.
"Wildwater!" she said. "And what about your little son?" I asked further.
"You would be surprised!" she said and glanced at me
with spiteful rancour. I realized that she was remembering, above all,
the cobbler Achatius, and how something with only a few claws
when it is grappled with, will at least growl in one's memory.

When I offered her a cup of tea with rum, she said: "You can't imagine
with whom I've had to live ... To rid oneself of a sewer rat, ground glass
with bread might be good ... But, it remains an open question
whether a flea would freeze on a frozen dog ...
But the boy? He didn't freeze! Sure, he was a ragamuffin
born out of wedlock ... Only recently weaned off milk,
he already yelled so much that the light bulbs all but shattered to pieces ...
But, if I was to write a footnote, it would say
that he didn't play with others, didn't roam about. He was quite insightful
and studied well; in a word: he planted a sedulous root
and lay low in wait for a better future ...
But, they made fun of him at school: they said
he was borne from a twice-begotten one in a bed of three
and they even flung cow dung at him ... a godling's nob may have
ninety-nine tentacles, but his had a plain one hundred!
Not long after, he started to wear a fur cap made from a mad dog.
Achatius implored St. Christopher, the patron of cobblers and tanners,
and betrothed the boy to the black-coat order. But this
puer oblatus raged uncontrollably. He then knocked about himself –
though the blows barely roused the fleas beneath a shirt.
He had always been weak ... I don't know anything more about him; he left
    me long ago ...
It's rumoured that he got married, but no children have come of it ...
There are reputedly men in the world
who feel as manly as a puppet in a nun's bed ..."

"Those nuns, I can't bear them either," she added
after an indignant silence ... "They are," I said, "the brides of Jesus."
"Yes," she said, rearranging her headscarf,
"but, I once saw some hens in Prague
in the convent yard; they were pecking at something near the church
entrance ..." – "They may have been Dominican hens;

there is such a breed, " I said … But she didn't want to hear me
and went on: "I go to church only on Good Friday …
That's when Pilate writes until the whole world trembles …
The graveyard wall is quite warm by then … You know,
one ought to die young … But I never loved,
even if written in ottava rima …
To die young … There isn't enough in that, and always when you want
to confide in someone, the secret council of the dead,
the council of the dead ancestors, is already in session.
And, lamentably, even for them it's not a land of milk and honey here …"

Contrary to antiquity, it is possible that even Apollo
comprehended the parable as a possibility and
thus he loved movement … As I gazed at her,
I told myself: be it just an embossment
on a funeral urn, on a stele or even on a collection box,
as a *form* it always aimed into space.
Had I spoken this aloud? She responded by saying
that I overly believed in a future, and this only because
I always stood a good inch behind everything.

"But you have forgiven, haven't you?" I asked her.
"Whom?" she said recklessly. "Not perchance
that amorous flute or those nightingale tonguelets?
In Idyllion de Majomensa you argue
that joy can only spring forth from love
and, above all, only from love without passion … But I
was young before my youth … I didn't love,
and therefore I couldn't love less by the truth of my hate …
Love!" – And she said it as if she wished for
Paolo and Francesca da Rimini to spit into a book …

Her voice sounded as though it came from a kind of
crease in her senses: lost in matter without flesh.
It reminded me of how ideas without eternity
only arise and thus merely measure mortality. –
However, it wasn't for the first time that I hadn't stood my ground.
I sensed that man, for all his wanting to escape delusion,
discovers the ephemeral. And for his wanting to capture
at least one part of what is real, he finds himself in his suffering …

VLADIMÍR HOLAN

I don't know why I still hoped then
that she – her appearance already mythos-centred –
might have proceeded from play into interplay
even if it had been an interplay without hope,
when there wasn't even a single hint
that she had a sense of balance and could thus have been in equilibrium with
    mystery.
I believe now that I merely hoped we wouldn't part like this
and that I could convince her that there was nothing here for nothing …

But we want to be all-encompassing without knowing how to embrace.
Could I have helped her somehow? Should I have kissed her hand?

I really don't care about time; I was always playing truant,
and there were always two of us who did so: a child and a poet …
And yet, ah, it was not the first time that I hadn't stayed for a test.
Yet again I was unable to catch what was not falling,
there where life is unveiling what it had not concealed …

But enough about that! It was necessary for me to leave … I didn't even
say goodbye to the old woman; that is how fast another desert
opened before me … A desert …
A lion was looking back at me, and I followed him.

(1951)

Martin of Orle, Yclept Mortmain

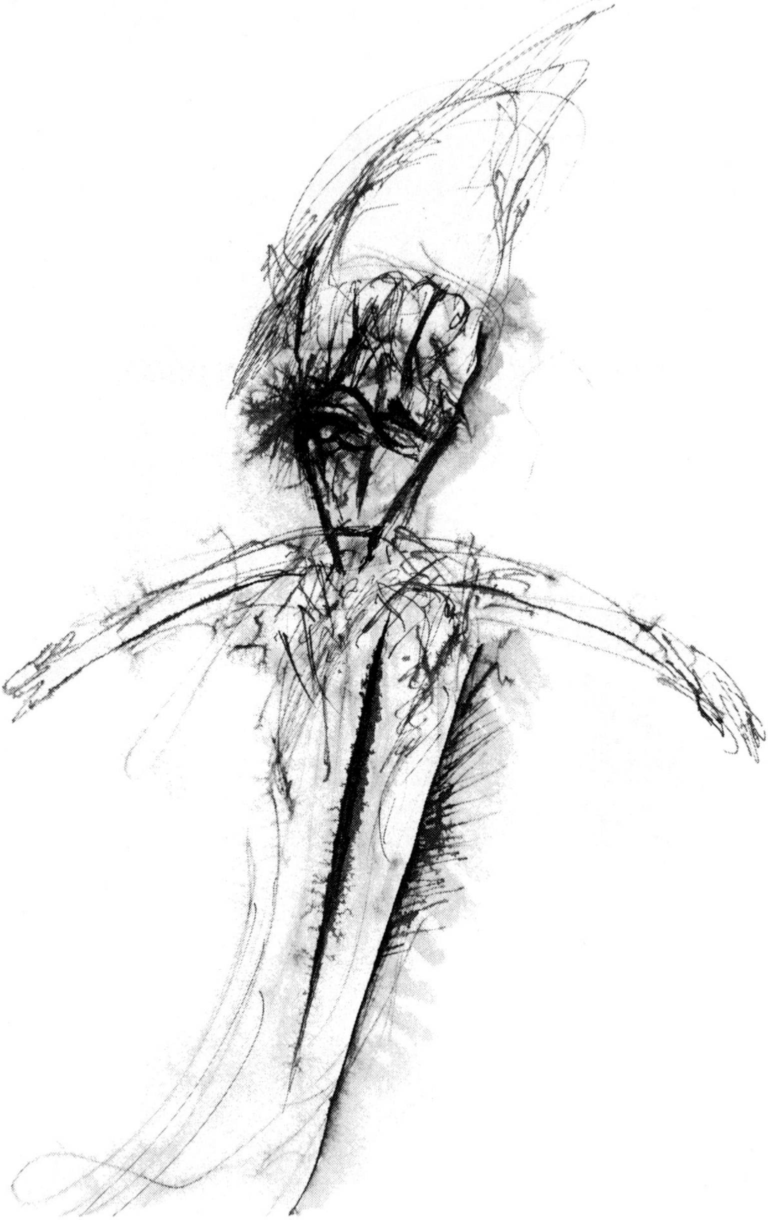

MARTIN OF ORLE, YCLEPT MORTMAIN

I met him, when he was no longer youthful,
at the Gohatagat manor where he served as a gamekeeper.
Several times I overnighted at his place.
They said of him (especially those finicky impotents,
who erstwhile had played the clarinet but who stopped
the instant their teeth fell out and thus lacked an *embouchure*),
that he, in his youth, had left the conservatory for a danseuse ...

If you guessed, then guess again, but I did not want to guess;
I revered him and I cleaved all the more to his narration about
how once, during his urban youth,
he had been hurrying from somewhere in order to catch the last night tram,
and how he had arrived on time but then let it drive off,
with a blissfully revengeful grin on his face
as though it concerned a hearse.
It was midwinter. It was madly cold,
and it would be unduly noble to claim that, as he gazed ahead,
he dismantled the city ramparts and then reassembled them again
merely by stepping forward without glancing back.
The truth was, it was from thence that he'd set out on foot into the
    countryside
so as to stay there for good ...

His small gamekeeper's lodge stood on a hill.
Enfolded on three sides by the woods' solitariness,
it opened at the front onto a pond with a hatchery
and warmed me with an immediate foreknowledge,
the foreknowledge that I had a friend ... I spent
one summer there with such ardour that in its deepest place
it remained timeless – and now I only see a blind horizon
that frequently has a piercing pain in its side:
for a moment the storm flashed heavenward,
only to disgorge later, somewhere above Godalming,
it's large intestine stuffed full with hailstones,
and as the mother of all thunderbolts mutinied with an uproar,
the thunderbolts slid down the trees.

Since the trees were broad-leaved and in groves,
something was always going on in there ...
Public broadcasting, which had already razed

both silence and song in the countryside,
had been forgotten by the oriole – that organ grinder at Eden's gate –
as well as by the horn beetle, the owl, the goatsucker,
the stray grass snake, the whimpering of a yew,
the horse with its ears turned back in truncated bliss
as it rubbed its flank against a maple tree,
the colchicums covered in gipsy dew, the song of a rooster
that follows a metric beat whenever the sun migrates
through the element of water or the meadows turn into hay,
or a stag dons its antlers:
all this condemned nearly everything
written in this century for being apocryphal.
And yet: if other people befoul the Universe,
why must I also see in the starlit night
a cowpat beset with flesh flies …

"You are right!" added the gamekeeper Martin.
"Let's go and drink to it!" … With pleasure, I replied
because I well know the despair that arises out of immoderate hope,
even if I (being still too young)
at first misunderstood his reticence. He never mentioned his wife,
who was by then already deceased … But one day,
when the stubble-field wind was smashing itself
against the soccer field barrier
coated with sparrows' blood, he told me:
"It's a good year for wine! … What a pity
that my soul only enters my body to sleep …
We had a little girl … At her christening (it was during the war
and even the church dust was whirled up by a jackboot),
at her christening, in precisely that dust
mixed with sunlight, I noticed a glimmer of bone on the organ keys
and an evening butterfly, the same one that many years later
would land fastidiously on a funeral cake …
I couldn't get it out of my mind, no matter what …
The girl was given a name … To give a name!
I had no idea what name to give because,
compared to God's creation,
everything here is just a replica … And so,
she was baptized Replica.
Replica, come here! Replica my darling!

MARTIN OF ORLE, YCLEPT MORTMAIN

Replica, look: this is a little ear, this a little nose
and this a shoe, a little shoe, and this ... But enough,
there's no need to weep over primroses
made conscious by the *brain* of spring ...
Of course ... however ... once, as she played alone
on the banks of the pond, she was pecked to death by a swan ...
I wanted to ... they reasoned with me ... I don't know ... What if, in truth,
fate glanced at a comedian's spoil sheet
and pulled the strings? ... Why then shouldn't I claim
that there are only four parts of the world?
Why shouldn't I measure a mountain's height with a waterfall?
Such direct insistence, but what a deviation!
Life really makes no sense ...
But, suicide is mutiny and I am no slave ...
Ever since then I no longer kill swans;
I always only bring them down and *always only in flight,*
and always only on my way to the lake
when the wind is computing, from the waves' knuckles,
the number of days the water has until full moon ...
What do I care that two of them fell into liquid manure!"

Love-crossed and then forsaken, lovers
need not see themselves in the absence of the self
when everything vanishes and yet is fitfully apprehended,
like a face wiped with a towel full of holes ...
I understood well, both the weighty glance
and the dipsomania of the gamekeeper Martin ...

"Elixirs of immortality! Why something that is liquid?"
he used to say ... "It's only a particular *frowziness*
that makes slivovitz so delicate!" And he kept the slivovitz
buried in the four corners of his district.
There were four small cellars, each beneath a thunderstone,
and he rolled the stone back four times a day during his errands, and
he rolled it back jealous of his lack of time and looked around
with eyes conversant even with that which is non-human.
He rolled it back in such a way that, close to the fifth hour in the afternoon,
he was high as the sky ... I do not know
where he kept his head if his breast bone was below the world,
but only then was he brave enough to shout into the clearing

at some thieving hags until they took to their heels,
and only then did he collect the poachers' snares
or chase out the illicit cattle
that grazed on acorns in the oak woods ...

"I like boozing very much! ... But, never in anger!"
he used to say ... "When I have a drink, I feel
as if only now God had come into existence ...
and as if nature's images,
painted during my boozing, were just a tribute
to Eve at the very moment she fell from the tree in Eden ...
And, since poverty does not know what belongs to it,
I become subsequently even more lonely,
but somehow with a blessed spirit,
for I also sing and sometimes converse while I'm at it ...
Why, I wouldn't last if I weren't allowed to sing ...
So what if I happen to swerve about
like a horse criss-crossing its front legs!
It's as if I'm washing my doleful memories out of myself
and feeling my youth ... Alas,
a little later, after a mere flee-tumble of my mind,
I feel a knot on the crown of my head,
as if from the handkerchief used to bind the chin of the deceased ...
Thereafter, self-regard sneers at self-hate,
and my eyes, with their sanguineous whites,
are my night birds searching for something
and yearning for a haystack on fire ..."

But, he died rather badly ... One night in December,
Martin Mortmain happened to sit with the mayor of Godney.
They had been drinking since three in the afternoon when the sun
had been, like erstwhile above ancient Egypt,
no more than a ball of burning dung.
They drank some lordly drink, not brandy. There was
a heck of a lot of it because the mayor,
though he suffered from constipation, was no miser.
"Uh-huh," he said, "there are females, as we know, who will drink this stuff
with rosemary to make themselves barren ...
While others will sit on a locked padlock for that ...
But, there are also women in childbed who'll turn up

at the hop!" ...

Then they started playing cards ...
But, because the gamekeeper had a golden hand
even as he cut the cards, the mayor moved on wearily
to more recent times: " Imagine!" he said. "It happened
at the fair in Gahatagat! Imagine a good-looker,
a very beautiful counterfeit!, who
just happens to be leaving the hotel toilet that you're entering,
and you find the toilet seat's still warm from her ...
Well, of course it was Dorothy-fragrant soap! ... Woman!
I know only a peon's hole and two blown eggs!"
"You talk," commented the gamekeeper, "as if your children
were bastards!"
"Merde!" the mayor replied, "but, you do remember
that Italian prisoner during the First World War?
His name was Armando, and when he ploughed he shouted
at his team: 'Oxen, walk if you please'!"

"You're just unbraiding cobwebs with a butcher's finger!"
said the gamekeeper and also wanted to add that one loves in vain ...
but the heartfelt obscenity of the mayor
would have only embodied itself more, the more he had solemnly sworn.

The whole of the mayor's racy monologue
brought to mind a boy drawing a woman's womb
on the dusty mudguard of a car ... The car starts moving
and arrives in another town ... Another boy there,
without needing to wet his finger,
adds to it a man's member ...
And, perhaps, the car will have to
set out that same evening on a long trip,
just so new dust
would veil both those drawings ...

Around one at night (why hurry,
you may even spend the night here!), the mayor complained
(with a trembling voice, as though he were concerned
about the upkeep of a werewolf) that no way
could he get the hog out of the pigsty.

VLADIMÍR HOLAN

Not desiring so much to shorten the moment as to change it,
the gamekeeper Martin, yclept Mortmain, made a bet
that he would force the fatling out and the mayor would kill it ...
"You know, it only seems to concern Heliogabal!" he added deliriously,
"I'll have a word with him and he'll take the hint! ... Besides:
no pain, no gain!" ... "Pell-mell!" the major
ascertained with enthusiasm and unclenched his jaw ...

Martin threw on his fur-coat and the mayor,
just in his butcher's apron, gripped the axe
and both of them ... off to the pigsty ... They tottered out
of a bacchic warmth into the yard ...
The moon was full ... Even the frost had a bosomy glow
in its voice ... For a while the drunkards heaped the air
six feet high, and when they, beneath the glimmer
of lascivious icicles, had done justice to Falstaff's kidneys –
they booted off the hatch and the gamekeeper crept in on all fours.

A croaky fight resounded; the grunting in particular
winked at the mayor's consciousness,
and the purring pulse changed into an impatient outline of what
he well-nigh wished to see
but which, invariably, retained its head start into the void ...
And then, suddenly noticing
a bristly lump spilling out the hatch (the gamekeeper, in a hurry,
had tossed on his fur coat fur side out!) –
he struck with his axe ...

That chop to the backbone (and perhaps it was
precisely into the little bone of *luz* which, according to a rabbi's fable,
is indestructible) was for the gamekeeper
deadly even if, as is commonly said,
it was only the consequence of his fate, the fate
 (that cardsharper!) which also had marked with a sharp nail his card ...

Martin Mortmain! ... He had been my friend ...
However, his funeral was glorious ... To this day I can see
how, on the preceding evening, all the villagers
hurriedly tidied the graves of their beloved

so that the next day no one would slander them,
and then, close to All Souls' Day,
they'd throw the rotting wreaths from the graves they most revered
onto the nearest graves they most disregarded ...

(1951)

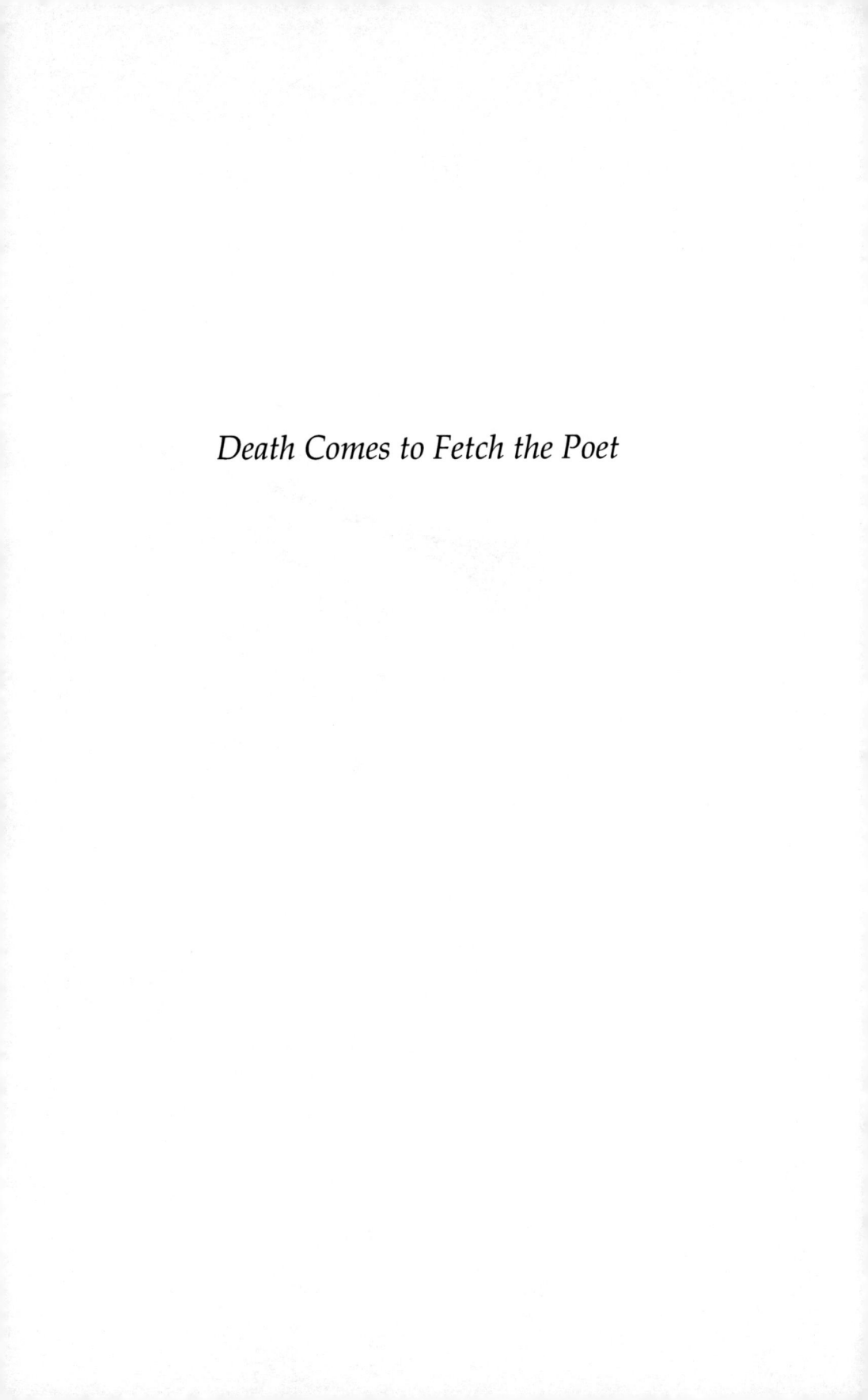

Death Comes to Fetch the Poet

DEATH COMES TO FETCH THE POET

Only just born, and already everything was decided ...
And the one who had decided, felt joy.
Such a child, with its entire being,
can live only entirely in freedom
and for freedom. One could say:
through joy towards pain, which cannot be measured.

Already as a boy he played truant.
He never knew what date it was
and so was always embroiled in some barbarian adventure,
and he scrawled upon every wooden barrier he came across
a challenge in block letters: *For dancers only*,
and those who read it wanted to become children again
and wanted to believe in a future after death ...
This now was his laugh, as if Dionysus
had always arrived on his donkey ...
Since he could never say to anything: what do I care!
and since in poesy there is no dispensation from anything,
don't expect him to be dutiful.
Even as a telegraphist he would run off
at the instant of an "important" message,
and you, displeased, would see him
promenading with a girl on each arm.
You cannot understand, since few of you have ever drunk,
even once, straight from a fountain.

Faithful to the inconstancy of life,
he doesn't stay anywhere for long; everywhere the ground shakes under him.
This doesn't mean he despises you,
but it is with him as it is with a fire's flame:
he warms you by fleeing from you ...

Moreover, if during an entire year most people
are sighted only on All Souls' Day,
he loves his land and the dead so incessantly
that the living cannot, in fact, catch sight of him;
the living who know him by name only,
which demands nothing else
(il est né aveugle, poete) – perforce like Thamyras
who was vanquished by the Muses and blinded,

perforce like Steichoros who was blinded because he insulted Helene –
the living who place upon the graves of the dead
a flower vase, not a vase for flowers.

This doesn't mean that he disregards you,
or that he disregards your fear of suffering
from which he always keeps a striking distance ...
Even if your soul were hairy,
he has always suffered for other souls
and sometimes has even spoken on their behalf,
he who is expected to come out of himself and still love,
he who isn't always present.

When the clock strikes midnight, he begins to live wholly
by the astronomical clock ... Do not hold it against him
that he is wakeful at night, just because you are asleep and because Jesus
    Christ
was born during the night ... Tell me, who else would sing and beg
at prostitutes' doors? And who else would plead
for the absolution of their debts with precisely those
who had refused to lend even a penny for nappies?
And who would sin at an hour when
you find yourself beneath the world, while overhead you are just heavily
    sighing?
And who would, with his heart, spirit and soul,
accept dreams that you, still asleep, have refused,
and who would open the door to the mailman who makes his rounds only
    at night?

And do not hold it against him that his night
is longer than yours: he delays himself sometimes
by muffling the clocks' hourly chime with his hand,
so it won't wake you;
another time a sleepless night is spent by a mother
in the requiem chapel for the little heart, which they will carry to tomorrow's
    christening.
There are, after all, newborns destined for death who are christened sooner,
just as there are adults destined for baptism who die later.

And don't hold it against him that he fled his wedding

DEATH COMES TO FETCH THE POET

so he could celebrate the beauty of all women. There is nothing to vindicate him,
save the fractured bones of Ikaros and those he won't show you ...
His selfishness possesses, as its fundamental measure,
a dereliction that is crueller than his poverty.
O you, who do not believe in and therefore cannot provide anything on credit.
O you, who would gladly force him to
scrawl on the walls of hell so as to praise poverty,
when after all he is here for poverty, pain, consolation and the celebration of all women
(perforce like Orpheus, who was clawed to pieces by the women of Thrace).
O woman, whom I first saw coming out of
the house of Lazarus; oh yes, I understood
that only by leaning against the earth could we suffer vertigo,
but the beauty of a woman entrusts itself only to the sadness of a man.

Just a few moments later, I saw you
in the great hall of Bezdez castle,
where they used to lower a basket with bottles of white wine
into the well to speed up the cooling for the king.
But at sunset, the jealous king approached you, unsuspecting,
from behind and covered your eyes with the palms of his hands,
and you said: "But, my dear!" and called him by my Christian name.
Within an hour I was thrust into irons and soon after hanged,
as if the beauty of a woman could entrust itself only to the death of a man ...

A short time later I saw you in the kitchen at daybreak,
preparing beefsteaks (spreading suet
over the hindquarters of a lamb) and celery salad for our guests
who did not feel like going home.
You must have already been tired; but no,
through all your gestures you radiated such joy
that I said to myself: woman's beauty is only then beauty
when it inspires man with assurance. And I recalled my mother.

Another time I saw you in all my lascivious dreams and omens;
it was my lust that wanted to have you.
I started to drink first thing in the morning,
learning to keep silent while drinking wine,

and, as if I had killed someone,
I took refuge in the labial cottage pour voir Carmen,
and I waited that at least my friends would join me there; but they never came because I hadn't killed her.
Ah, I recognized what a mouth is and what lips are
and what a bottle of cognac knocked over by a word is
and an upright bottle of soda that silently fizzes
while the floors are already being swept, though the windows are closed.
I recognized what a woman's pity is: because to possess her
does not mean to understand her ...

This may be why Menandros
used to visit Aigina for the orgies
and Isthmos for the mysteries ... But I
saw you again only quite recently:
not as the pale blue Venus' vein
but simply you ... After you had put the child to sleep,
you said: "So, you have returned? How nice of you, but don't brood over it now!"
I began to cry, for I saw that she no longer was beautiful –
but she was patient and humble –
and that it was only because of her patience and humbleness
that I was still able to sing about beauty, the beauty of a good nurse,
about self-sacrifice and, thus, about her greatness and a man's melancholy.

And don't say that a poet exaggerates everything;
in childhood everything looms larger, after all,
and the biggest truth is like God! –
O you, who do not believe and therefore cannot provide anything on credit!
O you, who have no time while He has so much of it!

Even this is his laugh, since it is hopeful – not so much a laugh now, as only a smile,
though a smile no longer juvenile
and yet still arising from his heart's belief.
He is not defending himself, even if to his dishonour
he had to sell his hat and a ring inherited from his father –
it is the bitter smile of a man as lofty as
a game of poesy played with a lunatic in the presence of life and death –
it is the scarified face of a man who knows

DEATH COMES TO FETCH THE POET

that even God, before too long, regretted that He had created man ...

Without suffering, there is nothing here.
Even a vineyard *bears* wine.

Difficult is the road from Trampletown into Sailhill ...
I will tell you a short story, ad excelsa:

It was around St. Anne's day, when water blooms;
it rained and was coldish. I was already tired
and hungry ... The gravel under my feet and the forest on the horizon
inspired me with the hope that I would find a glassworks nearby.
I found it, warmed myself, ate my fill and slept.
As I was leaving, I met a woman at the door
who cried into her apron and told me not to go through the woods.
But, there was no other way for me, and so I moved onward
without asking her why I shouldn't ... I would find out before long.
After barely an hour on the road, I noticed that I was utterly alone,
and that, as yet, I hadn't roused a single woodpecker nor a doe or even the
    paw of a weasel,
and that I was enclosed by a kind of blind rustling,
which contracted my throat, by the rustling of a thousand unfolded winglets
that immediately ceased whenever I stopped ... It was then that I beheld
a whirling stillness, one known to us from paintings on pillars ...
This painting was in black and white ... But, as soon as I stepped forward,
all over again began the rustling, the anxiety and
the squinting cloudiness, which forced me to illuminate everything with my
    own eyes.
Suddenly I fell into a dead past and sensed
the apex of my weak memory, the memory that by sunset
should restore my awareness of how I'd lost my way and that it was the
    nun moths
who trembled in the forest and quivered within me.
And the forest began to reek of a roguish desire ... I never liked
the smell of lilac. It always seemed to me as though its sleeve
was being filled at a bar by the hand of a night guard,
who watches over all the deceased flowers.
And, in truth, I could already smell
that persuasive deadliness, which wanted to be inhaled by a noseless one.
Moreover, there was also a certain senility in it, which was growing

evermore younger – and all the trembling moments of those nun moths
(the moister the air, after yesterdays' rain, the more harrowing the rustling!)
were changing into an existence that would never cease ...
And it wanted death, not only the death of a tree but also yours,
and it bumped into your face with the docility
a cube would posses if it were round ...
How it resounded! How alone I was!
If only I had a love letter in my pocket!
If only I was leading a horse by its reins! If only there was
a bear's ear here or the little ear of a squirrel
or a hunted deer's saliva
or a woodpecker, because the nose does not matter to the woodpecker
    after all ...
But, such nothingness, such nothingness! Only a rustling
rising endlessly upward
towards the Melusine in the crematorium's chimney.

Once I saw a beehive burning, set ablaze by someone
whom they could never convict, because human malice
is so furtive ... I felt in those sylvan places,
where sorcery was practiced, a malice that was palpable
and that warmed those nun moths.
They battered my face, spat at it, defecated and copulated there;
they reeked and rustled, millions and millions of them, and nobody, not even
God, would ever destroy them,
not even with a spark from the flint of His omnipotence –
they were so self-confident, so deceitful and malicious.
They despised even Satan, out of whom they had arisen;
they had made themselves for themselves and, consequently,
rendering someone soulless means to murder them ...

Without a safeguard against such malice,
I sensed that I would soon die, that I had loved too little
and that those nun moths possessed something (though wrong side out)
that I've never had: patience ...
I realized, too, that though we still have here and there
forests and groves, we no longer have *wildwood* ...
And now even these forests will perish because within them
all our promises have reached a merciless arrangement ... And frequently,

DEATH COMES TO FETCH THE POET

    from that time on,
I have asked myself whether I would want to live anew again ...

A poet's fame always speaks in the third person,
for it barely registers on the scale of God ...
A poet is far-sighted into the present, which was the only reason why
Quevedo predicted the Spanish colonies' fate,
why it was Seneca who prophesized the discovery of America
and Chlebnikov the year of the Russian revolution,
while forty years earlier Virgil foresaw the birth of Christ the Lord ...

A poet's every wish is fulfilled;
no wish can be granted to him!
Every book is an unfinished book,
as though one would say: behold my future,
for it concerns a library of paupers.

And if every saint, and in fact every priest, were Simon Cyrene
(because he helped Christ carry the cross),
let this simile be a self-presumptuous one:
the hot-tempered heart of a poet
throbs, above all, in short stories;
his sympathy pays in bloody sweat
for each penny's worth of fate,
and when the soul is called
by the simplest things,
he is already near them, with them, *dutiful*.
He affirms their mystery through his vision;
the knowledge of events means nothing to him,
nor does science, that cow on stilts –
for if his concern is knowledge, then it is the knowledge of the heart.
He places large canvases of history
beneath his attic window,
opened perchance to the Mycenaean layers of Troy.
Ben Johnson observed the battle between the Carthaginians and Romans
on his big toe –
but within those Mycenaean layers, I was touched and moved to tears
by the dust scattered into dust
and within that dust by a baby's ivory rattle,
which surely was for a little girl

because I favour baby girls.
It was the smallest rattle in the world.
Oh surely for a little girl. I saw her;
I saw her alone, all alone
in a cradle; I saw even her little left hand and, on that little left hand,
one little nail illuminated by the kitchen fire,
by a real fire that heats only because it flees;
she was there alone, all alone,
and so pint-sized and thin, as if she'd eaten crickets' musical notes,
but her eyes were so sorrowfully attentive
that the poet, out of the greatness of his love,
could in this world see only through his tears ...

Later, it was not at all easy to find for that girl
the smallest ring in the world. But they found one
and, for the groom, a pocket bible ...
Already I regretted that it rained on their wedding day.
Their carriage passed a low wall behind which a brute
was flaying a carcass ... The wedding horses, with blindworms' eyes
and with nostrils opened by the earth's clef,
shivered and balked ... It was necessary to lash them,
even lead them by their reins ... The road continued
through a poppy field and later through a gorge, which
forced upon the river a flowing crease ... But before
they had arrived at the church, the bell's heart had broken off ...
A rather bad sign! But both had been mated by force ...
They had been told: Whatever is fated, to whomever, will ...

A poet who doesn't know himself, let alone his passion,
can only become silent here
since fatalism is too irresponsible
for him not to blame his first disappointment
on fate, coincidence, resignation, apathy ...

Pleasure, laughter, woe and song –
where have you gone? ... Given that just now, on Good Friday,
people believe in treasures being opened and in the spirits drying their
    money,
on the ninth day desperation will be like nine millstones around your
    neck ...

DEATH COMES TO FETCH THE POET

On such a day (which could, given one's fate, take many years),
even time – which once used to hide inside the just-being-written poem –
wants already now, already now, its death,
and the poet has nothing that an eye could withstand ...
And it was precisely then that his fellowmen allowed him to
be dragged by the lice into a horse pit ... Even the wind had died down ...

Will you, God, take mercy on him,
so that he perseveres and does not kill himself?

(1951-1952)

A Letter

A LETTER

My lady, I've heard that to stop a swan
from flying away, one clips the first pinion
on one of its wings so that the wings' asymmetry
will hinder it from taking off. Fortunately you are not a swan,
and without any forefeeling of what was done to you,
you just are; you live on this earth; I saw you;
you are beautiful; you laugh; you like art and this at your own risk;
you've written to me and your letter was as short as a papal breve;
you are full of character but are wrong about snakes:
a poem is not a novelty tailored to fit people's tastes.

I would drink even from a death bell …
And, if you were an innkeeper, I would request from you
three litres of wine, marked on a slate with a thin black line.
And if you were a chatelaine in a fort or on a farmstead,
I would request a pint of gin from you,
and after a venial silence stolen from here or there,
I would tell you what I am ashamed of on Spy Wednesday
when we only see time's rear end …
No, a poem is not a novelty tailored to fit people's tastes.

A scion wedged into a coppice shoot yields only kindling.
Only a pruned tree has a head,
but the apple tree has a crown.
The bloom runs to seed and regenerates the apple tree by *bearing fruit* …
It is still early … How beautiful this evening is
on which I am replying to you and keeping,
for the approaching night, all the white spaces
alongside those secretly opened letters.

Am I worthy of clemency? Answer me, you woman out of a woman!
I have no power over my body, unless I am a false Orpheus.
I take the stairs, two steps at a time –
all of us were children once.
No, a poem is not a novelty
tailored to fit people's tastes.

An angel and a demon – a chord to a chord –
they converse with us clearly.
A more peculiar thing is *a bird on the ground.*

VLADIMÍR HOLAN

You say that I am a maniac, and you laugh into the cloudy heights.
Miraculous are the mysteries of a virgin's delights;
but you are a woman, and I know what a fenced garden is
and that, at the end of August,
a daisy closes its blossom already by about five,
and a rose alters its voice.
My lady! I have desired for a long time now
to compose a prayer for my readers.

But, I know what a walled garden is, la finta semplice,
and a man with a Browning in his hand:
he is jealous of anyone and is lanced even by his own bile.
Let him fight then, with whomever he wants;
he won't force me to say otherwise –
though I have to admit that Rome only warred with Hannibal
so that Plautus could learn Punic.
But, I saw a weir broken asunder by ice,
and I can see his heart and the same will happen to it.
In the meantime, let him read a novel, one that smokes cigars.
My heart is far more cruel, my lady.
I have desired for a long time now
to compose a prayer for dead poets.

Once I am alone, even goodliness means nothing.
You did not block my path; you appeared
illuminated by a lantern suspended
from the statue of Johann Nepomuk,
but soon after, someone shot through the lantern
and it was extinguished.
You took off your soiled ladies' shoes
and fled. I then heard voices
on the margins of my lids,
and I recalled how camel manure and Rachel's mendacious bleeding
had sufficed for the concealment of idols –
I have desired for a long time now to compose a prayer
for the mountain meadow and for the mirrors of disconsolate women.

You, my lady, do not need to cover
the contours of your voice with words
warmed up inside your throat.

A LETTER

When I hear you, I do not consider
who had dug a hole in the heavens above us
just to fill one grave after another down below –
no, when I hear you, I remember
the ones who used to sing in the fields at the time of harvest.
But, what wonder:
I have desired for a long time now to compose,
in five tempests, a prayer for the vagabonds.

But now, as the evening wades through the saltbush,
and I do not give you an answer,
you ask me whether to decide means to feel joy.
Whenever I decided, I felt a knife in my heart,
for we fear suffering and we fear pain,
and with the whole of our existence we refuse stubbornly
to place ourselves into others' souls, to suffer with them and for them.
We are more likely to take an interest in a grain of barley discovered
inside the bricks of Dashur's pyramid
or in the excavations at Naga ed-Deir,
which merely establish the contents of
the digestive track of the deceased
buried sixty centuries ago.

Make no decisions, my lady; it would bring no joy. Just decide!
To leave before your time is no exaggeration,
nor self-destruction, nor suicide – be it a wilful one.
A pyramid is measured in ells for which, I know not why,
God ought to fulfil our every wish.
Do not ask me how free will
fits into fatalism. Surrender yourself to the will of God,
be it behind or in front of the door to mystery.
And, as you always hide behind it,
allow me to adore you.

The pressure of the night would play the organ,
if it's foot reached the pedals –
but, it is not yet fully grown ... And yet, I must
answer a different question of yours:
whether I believe in love ... My lady,
both with my first and with my last breath, I well know

that there are people who would be glad
if I apologized to them before I died.
I tell you, every love is unfortunate:
we are only beginning to adore, when lust arrives ...
We charmingly dispute the wall
that divides us, and then we lean against it.

A mosquito pillar that supported the sky collapsed long ago,
but the molehills remain.
A four-edged horn stone, carved at chisel's width into a dekahexahedron,
marches through moonlight's cubism ...
What might you be doing? I hear your dress; I think about your complexion;
I live with it outside of holy wedlock and without regard for the
    spectators.
Even a gravestone can be a pillory.
It isn't my fault that love has been turned into
a novelty tailored to fit people's tastes.

Isn't someone drawing you just now
with charcoal from Virgil's grave?
Nighttime carried across by a woman's nakedness
into a nightdress is ignoble.
Do you also see me? Do you at least remember me?
I am the death mask taken during my life,
hence the double likeness.
Separation feeds insanity
out of a wombful of femininity.
From the first cock's crow until morn,
the beginning is lost in God; the end is not the goal ...
From the first cock-crow until morn,
can blessedness despair?
I weep with gladness that you exist.
What am I going to do Anno ... die Veneris post S. Luciam?
An electron dances on a tantalum thread;
lovers emerge from the yellow part of a bar
and from the red part of flirtation:
"My little fool," she whispers to him
while on her neck glitters polished grit from the stomach of a grouse:

"My little fool, it's only a matter of a few days.

A LETTER

No, I am not a prioress, so I will write to you
on paper handmade by the forest wasps.
I know, I know, do not keep reminding me
that a tree is anywhere where space sleeps with time.
I will write to you, top down,
and will stop where you love me ..."

A dawn song under your window makes me bashful:
so many windows, but nobody fears beauty.
Likewise, my self-doubt with its yearning to adore
has thus far always overthrown my tearfulness ...
How starkly the moon shines upon drowned water!
Only the saliva beneath nature's elemental tongue
could dissolve a sleeping pill;
but, nothing stirs ... Even saints
had moments of thirstiness. I ought to
go to church: holy water, it is said, lasts
seven years without spoiling.

"When you distance yourself towards me," perhaps that is love ...
Even deviation is unavoidable ...
I knew a beggar who went from house to house
as if he were inviting guests to a ball.
There is indeed a secret love that is the least protected:
for it is the creatures dearest to us
who are snatched from us ...
Who escorted the souls of the dead? Hermes,
the god of thieves ... "Come, my dear,
we'll warm each other up." Even this might be love,
even this might be love so long as there is time,
quasi una fantasia ...

Dusted with pollen from the pine trees in bloom,
I approach you in a golden cloak.
To be liked by you is self-love.
A drunken old woman stops me at the priests' compound
and stretches out a trembling hand.
It is, in fact, not a hand but
its secret version, for the old woman
was afraid that I could inveigh against her.

I lead her away to her lodgings. I see poorly.
I always see poorly when a horse cries.
The old woman's hands are cold,
and she shivers all over. I go down with her to a tavern
and order tripe soup for her. But, she refuses
and only accepts a cup of black coffee.
And what do I care about LouisXV's syphilis;
what do I care about Democritus' atomism;
I have seen human hearts trampled to pulp,
those human hearts that were the most concealed …

"We still have to cross another river,
and then I'll seek alms again," mumbles the old woman
and, light-headed with the heat, she drifts off to sleep.
What am I to do? You can't drink away pain.
I order gin. I sip it on an empty stomach towards the grave.
I disregard the water clock –
for a long time now, we've been measuring the years in tears.
It would be delightful to hold a feast for an angel,
but how unbearable it would be if an angel were our host!
I sense that the old woman is my host,
even if she is snoring and looks like
the witch from Thessaly
just before the lunar eclipse.
I order gin; I smoke;
I broke an ashtray on the head of the dance of swing.
Everything remains in boxes at future's railway station,
as the progressivist used to say while sitting in the Hereafterhouse,
that drudge who used to cough up blood
and who, just before he died, in his attempt
to prove the existence of prematurity
thrust a knife through a friend's back
into his atrium, as if he were a fatling –
yes, there is such a thing as a scientist's probability
and a poet's parable. Tombstones
are lithographed. No, life is not
a novelty tailored to fit people's tastes.

The old woman snores from a sensitivity to the alcohol
she'd imbibed on my account.

A LETTER

That is how the moon walks across lakes;
that is how the sun does not walk across deserts –
near the upper end of a ternary smokiness
the gamblers' shouts rise to the hair.
The origin of one's hands is not concealed;
how placid is such a limb, but add the load of just one squirrel
and the limb will sway blissfully,
especially if it looks like rain.
Only we, given any pretext,
will go after the blood and milk of a deflowered virgin –
that is how self-confident we are within the quagmire of sudden vanishment.
Will-o'-the-wisps illuminate the soul, trapped in limbo
between appearance and name
upon a frame without canvas,
but there is nothing within earreach, nothing that could prompt
or provide a raft's calm in the midstream of appearances;
we are everything but not the centre.
A recollection stomps: it is Lomonosov
fleeing Marburk because of his debts.
And have I truly ever liked someone at all?
Had it not been just a spark, one that only darkened my passions' fall? …

I would never remember;
all my resolve has gone.
Have mercy on me, o Jesus Christ!
What was that mercenary's name, the one who pierced Your side?
I would never remember,
but I implore the living God that I may achieve salvation,
because I am a big sinner – You know it!
Longinus dances rumba with Helene
as though his feet were deleting Faust's prescriptions,
and their souls reek of bile. Later, they go to a taproom bar,
and while they are eating they share a spoon and a set of false teeth,
before opening cans of boneless sleep.
They talk, and into hollow reason penetrates a lascivious tongue.
Mater verborum remains silent.
The old woman snores; her arms are crossed.
O human hearts! You don't play, you don't pay and yet you still win
misery, which seeks punitive damages against you.
O human hearts! Indivisible is the sum of your ruin,

and out of the overcropped land you will emerge empty-handed ...
Only evil continuous to be fruitful
even though long ago Hor chopped off Sutech's testicles.
People also kneel, but only for mating,
and they presume – not while loving but only while making love –
that a seed which lies sideways
can silence the creaking of the gates to hell.
What time could it be? I hear footsteps in the street;
perhaps they are the footsteps of a priest who, even on the day
before his death, still goes out to celebrate Mass.
Such a day surely dawns with a harshness
that transforms the night into a mere ceremonial visit,
while within my mouth grows
an alcoholic aftertaste of unexorcized clouds.
It seems I heard a hammer strike iron.
Yes, blacksmiths must get up early in the morning
because they forged the nails for Christ our Lord.
Having considered this, I pray again
that God be merciful to us,
for we all despicably helped
to forge those nails.
Our spirit has fallen out of truth for good.
Who today would remember the quivering lips of Virgin Mary?
No, pain is not a novelty tailored to fit people's tastes.

The old woman is asleep. She now sleeps silently, that is to say: alertly.
With those like her it's always about seeking Proserpine,
while I already hear the tufted titmouse
as it gives the whole park an airing.
And the children, too, are shouting, fighting and arguing,
but it is always and again a little girl
who is crying. Il piano di Eva ...
(1953)

Escape to Egypt

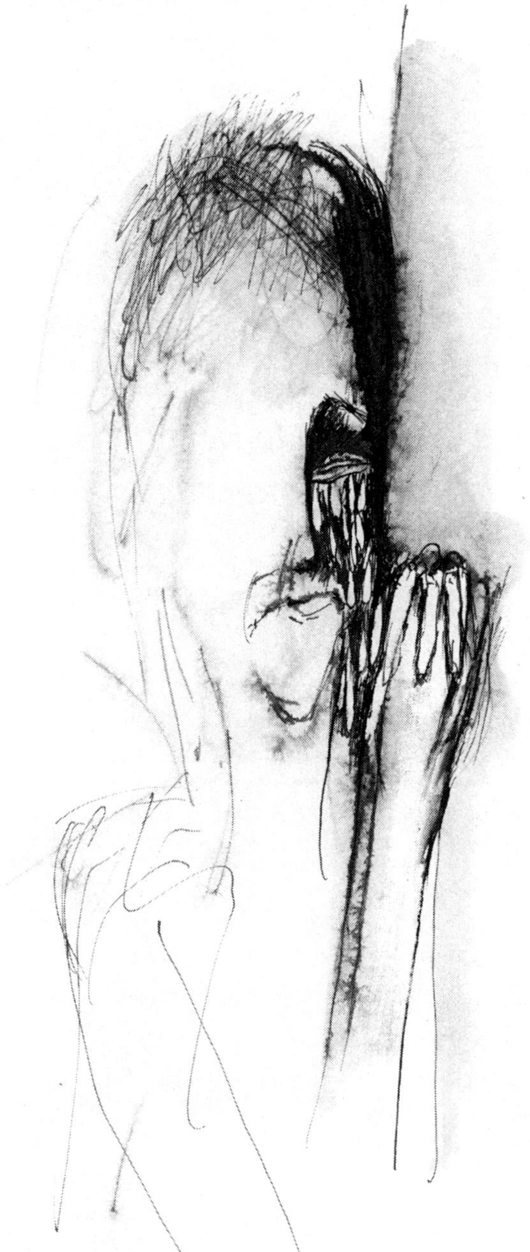

ESCAPE TO EGYPT

Woe befalls the nation ... I, too, could talk
about an evening dawn or just about
the soot from the fire of poesy ...
My God! The script of those unfinished letters
affixes fear onto the envelopes.
Duodrama is one ... What about pure play
and hence the children? Who can save them now
from that foul and lewd force, which is much less than
Satan but more than all the satanists?
The falling down of our whole nation's life
into servitude and untruth and murder
is merely the consequence of our sins,
where blindness may despair in the heart's eye ...

Again it is night, an unceasing night –
indeed, an uninterrupted reversion
of our sleep – and on this night I recall
what I once saw behind a hawthorn fence.

It was in a village ... Perhaps in August.
Swallows had nested for the second time.
It thundered in the woods: blowflies were swooping
to disturb a stag. It must then have been
September or October, for the morn
already reeked lightly of horseradish.
"My entire life, I was never in need of
more than two winter coats!" uttered the blacksmith
and then ruffled his hair nonchalantly,
as if wanting to warm his fingertips ...

A newt crept through the sand; many believed
that it could bring to ruin entire nations ...
And on the green, which you would not have noticed
if it had not been bespattered with birds'
droppings, a blackbird silently began
to colour his winglets with elderberries ...
The geese, smooth because freshly plucked, now quivered
and looked at the housemaid who had deplumed them
and gaggled about how bad that witch was –
but without that witch life would be much worse ...

Girls, in plain velveteen, strolled from school;
the boys, in the meantime, cooked up some plan
amongst the peeling bronze of falling leaves,
and then, of course, as soon as they surmised
that the girls were nearing, they began
to put on airs and talk crudely like brigands –
a fitting testimonial to women ...

In the cottage beside the distillery
a sheep dog barked (floppy-eared dogs always bark);
in that cottage that pretty bride of yours
was getting dressed in the kneading trough,
while the groom drank "Jewish tears" on the sly ...

It is the wrong question whoso asks thus:
"O happenings, what happened?" For, it's not
the turn of an act but the very act
that's always unexpected, unforeseen ...

Again it is night, an unceasing night –
a cruel, uninterrupted reversion
of our sleep – and on this night I recall
what I once saw behind a hawthorn fence.

In a village ... Not the children, the housemaid,
the newt, the geese, the thrush, not even the smith
nor the bride became infixed in my mind ...
I remember no one but the old woman,
whom I only glimpsed later that same day
behind a hedgerow ... I saw her clearly then
but am too mealy-mouthed to sing about it.
Woe befalls the nation. She too could talk
about an evening dawn, or just about
the soot left behind by her fiery love.
And I beheld her, kneeling in it all,
and then she kissed once, twice, a thousand times
the baby's footprint left there in the sand ...

Silent, and like a blind man eavesdropping
behind the doors of symbols, I at once

recalled the knife grinder jolting along
through this town ... Not some Zagreus, the ancient,
from the hills; a mere Joseph or Andreas
calling at this old woman's house and, later,
taking away with him her daughter who
cradled a little baby in her arms.
Perhaps he was no knife grinder at all;
perhaps he just cleaned the Czech lions' cages
by candlelight in Mariazell
or else he eked out his meagre subsistence
by making frames for queen bees. Perhaps, too,
he merely existed and, in his profound grief
for his people, he often kneeled to pray
not knowing at all that only by kneeling
can the greatness of life acquire strength ...

When he came to collect his wife and child,
he remained with the old woman much longer
than he'd planned and even drank a cup of coffee,
since not everything had been prepared yet,
and he was, no doubt, already muttering
and later got angry ... A bumblebee
often feels angry too – though at the blossom ...

At the Roman opera, I saw a scene
where an old priestess or a prioress
lost her voice when she had to sing a cantus
for the arrival of the infant Jesus ...
It was so frightful! Frightful was the silence,
and it was frightful to suddenly hear
a spider's legs weaving behind the curtain ...

Likewise, the old woman Anna must have felt
when, just around five, Josef left her house
with her daughter and child ... Indeed, the plume
of the Holy Ghost is not usually
as snow-white as the soot was charred and voiceless
from the fire of goodbyes and farewells ...
Maybe we're here for penance, yet the sight
of a baby's diaper, forgotten but

still fragrant with today's urination,
the sight of a torn picture book, the sight
of a broken puppet, surpasses us ...
Yes, the love that once was still is. But what
she loved and still loves is suddenly absent
and unseen, yet insisting to be ...
As in a fugue: where the theme keeps returning ...

At the Roman opera, I saw a scene ...
Today, Bohemia has lost its voice,
and I *mustn't* sing about the evening dawn
or about the old woman's grief and how
she wept the whole night of all our nighttimes,
where blindness may despair in the heart's eye ...

It was a cruel night, an unceasing night –
an uninterrupted reversion of sleep –
which like the script of unfinished letters
affixes fear onto the envelopes.
Duodrama is one ... What about pure play
and hence the children? Who can save them now
from that foul and lewd force, which is much less than
Satan but more than all the satanists?
The falling down of our whole nation's life
into servitude and untruth and murder
is merely the consequence of our sins,
where vision may despair in the heart's eye ...

It was a cruel night, a night of desertion,
a night of banishment without good friends,
a night when only a salamander sang
in the fireplace, who it was believed
could destroy whole nations; it was a night
when it was the wrong question whoso asked thus:
"O happenings, what happened?" For, it's not
the turn of an act but the very act
that's always unexpected, unforseen ...

It has only seemingly dawned today ...
The old woman did not sleep through this night;

she hasn't slept for many, many years.
And when the time swept past the midday hour,
I noticed her behind the hawthorn fence,
but I'm too shamefaced to sing it out loud.
Woe befalls the nation. She too could talk
about an evening dawn, or just about
the soot from the fire of no return ...

Behind the hawthorn fence I saw her then:
how she kneeled upon the sand and then kissed
the footprint many times, uncounted times ...
It was a baby's footprint, her granddaughter's
so dear to her, who only yesterday
pattered about here barefooted and lively;
it was a footprint, an authentic death mask
of living little feet ... where are they now?

Sculptors sneer at plaster and rightly so,
and I, forgive me, I almost despise it
because bronze is herein closer to life ...
Though, forgive me, I've had nothing to do
with either the bronze or the old woman ... Always
I've been a friend of babies' unstuck feet,
a friend of babies' feet pattering about,
a friend of babies' feet waiting to be kissed.
I've had nothing to do with classicism –
I was terrified when that ailing singer
at the Roman opera lost her voice,
but she didn't swoon, she just clasped her hands
and, instantly, she knelt down unaware
that it only can be when we are kneeling
that we acquire true greatness in life ...

That old woman behind the hawthorn fence –
I barely knew her and I always saw
how heavily she walked or, as one says:
 "pounded the pepper of old age" ... But proud
she was and held her head quite high despite
her sixty odd years and her austere life,
for she always took part in the game of life

and wasn't one to just pretend, oh no!
And, she certainly had been domineering,
but in the sense of what is being sung
is the singer too ... Singing gave her joy,
and she sang even about, for instance,
the hussars or the Moravian shepherds,
and her voice was soft like a woman's breast,
like a breast of snow when feeding the spring –
songs brought her joy, as they did to the baby
who enjoyed listening to her, not knowing
how easily the sob of a song could
repudiate the "barking heart" of Homer.

And, with the girl's first hair she had padded
a needle case, which they forgot to take,
and she found it today and then remembered
the baby's hangnail, but it was quite small ...

The light, with a pain in its back, bends the air ...
One could say that the wind also bows down,
while a bird, concealed somewhere in the grass,
leaves it to the tree to find it ... We, too,
fall humbly to our knees and pray to God
to find us ... And you my Lord, as long as
you don't find us, we will with the old woman
kiss the baby's footprint left in the sand ...

(1955)